SCHOLASTIC

Week-by-Week Homework for
Building Grammar, Usage, and Mechanics Skills

MARY ROSE

NEW YORK • TORONTO • LONDON • AUCKLAND • SYDNEY
MEXICO CITY • NEW DELHI • HONG KONG • BUENOS AIRES

Teaching *Resources*

To Tom,

my best friend

and patient husband

SPECIAL THANKS TO VIRGINIA DOOLEY, MARIA L. CHANG, AND KATHY MASSARO

Editor: Maria L. Chang
Content Editor: Eileen Judge
Cover design by Maria Lilja
Interior design by Kathy Massaro

ISBN-13: 978-0-545-06406-4
ISBN-10: 0-545-06406-6
Copyright © 2010 by Mary Rose
All rights reserved.
Printed in the U.S.A.

1 2 3 4 5 6 7 8 9 10   40   17 16 15 14 13 12 11 10

Contents

✳ Introduction

A Note from the Author

In 2002, I wrote *Week-by-Week Homework for Building Reading Comprehension and Fluency: Grades 3–6*. Two additional versions followed for grade 1 and for grades 2–3. Soon after, I wrote *Week-by-Week Homework for Building Basic Math Skills*. These books have been so successful with teachers that I decided to add writing books to the mix. I started out with *Week-by-Week Homework for Building Writing Skills*, and now, I am happy to present another book that takes on writing skills, *Week-by-Week Homework for Building Grammar, Usage, and Mechanics Skills*. Once again, my goal has been to offer a book of proven homework lessons that have been used successfully by my fellow teachers and me over the last couple of years. I hope this book will also help you communicate with your students and parents in a very special and productive way.

Teachers have always had an abundance of math and reading activities to send home, but rarely in this format: a note to parents and caregivers, classroom practice sheets that serve as examples, and a parallel homework assignment that is easy and fun to complete. As parents and families read the tips on these homework pages, they will understand what you are trying to accomplish in the classroom, and they will be better prepared to provide support at home. What a great way to foster the home-school connection!

I hope you find this book helpful. If you have comments or questions, please contact me at **Marycath@aol.com**.

Mary Rose

How to Use This Book

✳ **Make a plan for using this book according to your curriculum and your students' needs.** Each of the six sections in the book targets a skill, and each section has five specific unit lessons. In general, the first lesson in each section is the easiest, and lessons progress in difficulty. You may want to focus on only one skill at a time—for instance, comma usage—and complete all five lessons. You may prefer to do the first lesson in each section, then the second lesson, and so on, steadily introducing lessons of increasing difficulty. Again, your curriculum, instruction time, and the needs of your students will determine which skills you teach and when.

✳ **Select homework activities only for skills that the children have already mastered.** Homework should be a review, not an opportunity for the parents to act as the teacher. The letters home and the sample lessons are helpful, but they cannot take the place of your expertise and your instruction.

* **Take advantage of the convenient assessments provided to guide your instruction.** These ready-to-use assessments can be given before you teach, to help inform you of your students' needs so you can best plan your instruction. Together with the Review at the end of each section, they can also determine whether students need additional practice and support.

* **Before teaching, read the Overview of the Skills.** This introductory section provides essential information about the target skill and offers examples and suggestions for teaching the skill. Conduct a solid but brief mini-lesson based on this material.

* **Read the Teaching Tips.** Throughout the book, you'll find tips that will not only help you plan your instruction but also make it easier!

* **Complete the "We Did This in Class!" section of the homework pages. Do not skip this step!** These are short and easy to do. Their value is twofold: They ensure that students know how to do the assignment, and they serve as a model for parents and families of what the completed work should look like.

* **Discuss the assignments and the due date.** Before you send the pages home, make sure students understand the assignment and know when to return it to you.

Other Ideas for Using This Book

* **Give students the gift of time.** You might consider passing out the homework on Monday and expect it to be returned on any day up to and including Friday. Parents will love you for this, especially since most students are involved in sports activities, scouts, music lessons, or religious activities. Giving them all week to complete homework keeps the parents and children in control and allows them to decide which nights are the best homework nights. This is better than putting undue pressure on students and families on a certain night, and it is far better than listening to a litany of excuses about why the homework was not completed.

* **Display the rules of grammar and usage.** Designate a bulletin board for the grammar rules you are teaching. Whenever you teach a new skill, add it to the chart. You can make it more fun by adding a theme, for example: *1. Aunt Matilda says . . . put a comma between the city and state. 2. Aunt Matilda says . . . use a capital letter for the names of countries.* Even more fun and far more effective is to help children "own" the bulletin board by allowing them to take turns writing the rules and examples of the rules on the display.

Helpful Hints

* Fill in the "This homework is due at school on ____" space in PENCIL, so that you can erase this and use a new date next year.

* Fill in the due date before you make photocopies.

* Make two-sided copies. This will conserve paper, avoid the need to staple all of the assignments, and decrease the chances that these pages will be lost.

* **Save these lessons as student references.** Before you send the pages home, three-hole punch each page. After the papers have been returned to you and graded, do not send them back home. Instead, give them back to students to keep in a writing folder. This will allow them to refer to the lessons when they are writing so they have easy access to the rules of grammar.

* **Make assessment easy.** Because parents will offer a wide range of assistance to their children, instead of carefully grading each paper for every detail, consider giving full credit, partial credit, or no credit for these assignments. Skimming the answers will tell you if a student has actually acquired the skill you are working on. Indicate this in your grade book with a check, a check minus, or a zero. This will also help you determine at a glance which students might benefit from additional instruction and practice. At the end of the grading period, use a homework grade to help you decide the students' letter grade for the period.

Meeting the Standards

National Writing Standards

The lessons and homework activities in this book meet these writing standards set by the International Reading Association and the National Council of Teachers of English:

* *Students adjust their use of spoken, written, and visual language (e.g., conventions, style, vocabulary) to communicate effectively with a variety of audiences and for different purposes.*

State Writing Standards

State standards vary, if not in their intent, at least in their wording. The lessons and homework activities in this book meet the following standards, which are compiled from the benchmarks from several states.

* *The essay should follow the conventions of print, including punctuation, capitalization, and spelling.*

* *The essay should demonstrate a command of language, including precision in word choice, subject-verb agreement, and correct verb and noun forms.*

Dear Families,

Writing is one of the most important things that we ask students to do. It is often the most difficult, too. When writing, we have to remember everything we have ever learned about forming letters correctly, using language properly, organizing thoughts, and finally, about the mechanics of print, also called conventions. These mechanics include things such as knowing how and when to use commas, using quotation marks, assuring subject-verb agreement, and using correct spelling. It is a lot to think about while one is trying to get one's thoughts on paper.

Because print mechanics, or conventions, are so important, I will be sending home a writing homework assignment each Monday. Each assignment comes with a short note to you, the official "homework helper." The information in that box will refresh your memory of grammar rules and will guide you in helping your child complete this homework successfully.

You and your child will have until the due date indicated on the front of each page to complete the assignment. You are welcome to help your child, but remember that the child should be the one to actually write on the page. Be sure to sign the homework sheet before it is returned to school.

Please contact me if you have any questions concerning this project. The first homework is attached. Thanks for your assistance in making your child become the very best student he or she can be!

Sincerely,

....

Your child's teacher

Week-by-Week Homework for Building Grammar, Usage, and Mechanics Skills
© 2010 by Mary Rose, Scholastic Teaching Resources

Commas

One of the most misused punctuation marks is the comma. Help students grasp basic comma usage with the simple concepts in this section. Commas help us keep track of essential and nonessential information; avoid confusion by separating dates, numbers, places, and information in lists; and set the pace of a sentence by showing us when to pause.

Tip

Have students use a red pencil or pen so you can easily see their commas!

Overview of the Skills

Lesson # 1

Use a comma to separate city from state, and the day and year in a date.

Suggest that one way to tell where a comma might go is to notice where we naturally pause. For example, when talking about Omaha, Nebraska, we pause between *Omaha* and *Nebraska*. Likewise, when we say *October 12, 1492*, we pause slightly between *12* and *1492*. Here are other examples:

* *Thanksgiving falls on November 24, 2011.*
* *We are visiting my grandmother in Boston, Massachusetts.*

If the city and state or the date falls in the middle of the sentence, we also add a comma after the state and after the year.

* *In 2007, we went to Atlanta, Georgia, to visit my aunt.*

Lesson #2

Use a comma to separate words in a list, including multiple adjectives that modify the same noun.

Write the following on the board: "You can have chocolate cake angel food cake ice cream or pecan pie for dessert." Call on a volunteer to read the sentence aloud. Most likely, the student will read the entire sentence without pausing or will hesitate, uncertain of where to pause. Now, add a comma after *chocolate cake*, *angel food cake*, and *ice cream*. Have another student read the sentence. Ask students if they hear the difference.

Tell students that when writing three or more words (or phrases) in a list, we separate each word (or phrase) with a comma. Also note: in the sample sentence above, there will be a comma before the word *or*. This last comma is called a "serial comma." Explain that even though it is acceptable to leave out the serial comma, the preference is to include it.

* *I need to get bread, milk, and eggs from the store.* (preferable)
* *I need to get bread, milk and eggs from the store.* (acceptable)

When using more than one adjective to describe something, use a comma to separate the adjectives. *The large elephant walked toward us.* (no comma needed) *The large, gray elephant walked toward us.* (comma needed)

Lesson #3

Use a comma after an interjection, after an introductory phrase, or to set off a person's name when addressing that person.

Call on a student by name to do something. For example: "Maddy, please bring me the dictionary." Ask: "Where did you hear a pause in that sentence?" *(after the student's name)* Explain that when addressing a person in writing, a comma separates that person's name from the rest of the sentence. The name can also come in the middle or end of a sentence.

  * *Isn't that your bike, Tanika?*   * *If you practice, Jason, you'll make the team.*

Another place for a comma is after an interjection or exclamation. Point out the pause after the word *Oh* in the following example: *Oh, is that your new car?*

Demonstrate that a comma follows an introductory phrase:

  * *After dinner, you can have dessert.*   * *If we study now, we'll have time to relax later.*

Lesson #4

Use commas to set off appositives and words that are not essential to the meaning of a sentence.

When reading *Dinosaur Detectives*, my students saw this sentence: *The only way to be sure would be to find an embryo, or unhatched baby, inside the dinosaur egg.* When I asked, "What is an embryo?" no one could tell me. They did not recognize the appositive explaining the unfamiliar term. An *appositive* is a word or phrase that identifies or clarifies another word. Use the same sentence and ask your students what an *embryo* is. Show them that the answer is in the sentence and discuss how appositives function. Appositives can be found at the beginning, middle, or end of a sentence and are set off by commas.

  * *Our principal, Mr. Jones, will give out the awards.*

  * *The awards will be given by Mr. Jones, our principal.*

A sentence may also contain a word or phrase that interrupts its flow and is not essential to its meaning. Read aloud the following sentence: *Kelsey, however, had a good excuse for being late.* Note that if we take out the word *however*, the basic meaning of the sentence will not change. Explain that nonessential words or phrases, like *however*, *of course*, and *naturally*, are set off by commas, as in these sentences:

  * *Naturally, the rain delayed the game.*   * *The fans, of course, were not happy.*

Lesson #5

Use a comma to punctuate the greeting and closing in a friendly letter.

Display the letter at right. If necessary, review the parts of a friendly letter—the greeting, body, and closing. Call on a volunteer to point out each part. Guide students to notice that the greeting and closing are followed by a comma.

> *Dear Aunt Sarah,*
>
> *You'll never guess who came to our class today. It was the mayor! She congratulated our class for cleaning up the park. Isn't that cool?*
>
> *Your loving niece,*
> *Maggie*

Name _____ Date _____

Directions: Read each sentence, paying special attention to the blank spaces. Use a red pencil or pen to put commas in the spaces when needed. If a comma is NOT needed, do not put one in. NOTE: Make your commas large enough for the teacher to see!

1. I used to live in ___ Phoenix ___ Arizona.

2. Now I live in Salt ___ Lake ___ City.

3. Hey ___ Michael ___ would you like some candy?

4. St. ___ Patrick's ___ Day is always on March ___ 17.

5. The trick ___ of course ___ is knowing where to throw the ball.

6. Yes ___ you ___ may have some cookies.

7. We need to bring ___ crayons ___ scissors ___ and ___ glue ___ to math class.

8. My teachers' names are ___ Miss ___ Ridley ___ Mrs. Doerr ___ and ___ Mr. ___ Sheldon.

9. David ___ could you take Emily ___ fishing with you today?

10. December ___ 7 ___ 1941 ___ is a famous date ___ in our history.

11. I think our principal ___ Mr. Morris ___ is also a great ___ teacher.

12. I want to visit New York ___ New Jersey ___ Maine ___ and ___ Vermont.

13. My brother signed the letter ___ "Sincerely ___ George."

14. My cat is a big ___ fat ___ old ___ yellow stray.

Week-by-Week Homework for Building Grammar, Usage, and Mechanics Skills © 2010 by Mary Rose, Scholastic Teaching Resources

Dear Families,

The comma is one of the most misused punctuation marks in the English language. Sometimes they're scattered everywhere, as if it didn't matter where they landed. Whole books have been written about when and where to use a comma, but you will be happy to know we are going to focus only on comma rules that are appropriate for elementary school students. We will begin with these two easy rules.

*   **Put a comma between a city and a state.**
    (Camden, New Jersey; Dallas, Texas; New York, NY)

*   **Put a comma between the day and year in a date.**
    (October 12, 1492)

Since some of the questions on the homework may seem personal, please feel free to provide fictional answers to any of these. We are not seeking the information, but we do want your child to demonstrate that he or she understands the most basic uses of the comma.

Commas to separate city from state, and the day and year in a date

We did this in class!

Directions: Write a complete sentence for each of the following questions.

1. Where do you live? (Include city and state.)

   _____

2. Look at a book on your desk. Where was it published?

   _____

3. In what city and state does your favorite sports team play?

   _____

4. What was yesterday's date?

   _____

5. On what date did school start this year?

   _____

Name _____ Date _____

I. Directions: Answer the following questions by writing complete sentences. Pay particular attention to where the commas belong.

1. What is today's date? (month/day/year)

   _____

2. Where were you born? (city/state)

   _____

3. When were you born? (month/day/year)

   _____

4. What city and state would you like to visit?

   _____

5. When is Independence Day?

   _____

II. Directions: Look at the sentences below. Write "correct" if the commas are in the right places. Write "incorrect" if they are in the wrong places or missing.

_____ 1. Someday I hope to go to Mackinac Michigan.

_____ 2. My brother was born on October, 15, 1999.

_____ 3. The new mall will open on April 28, 2009.

_____ 4. My favorite vacation was our trip to St. Louis, Missouri.

· ·

This homework is due at school on _____ .

_____   _____
          Child's signature   Parent's signature

Comma Lesson #1

Week-by-Week Homework for Building Grammar, Usage, and Mechanics Skills © 2010 by Mary Rose, Scholastic Teaching Resources

Dear Families,

Many people, including adults, often get confused as to where a comma should go in a sentence. One way to figure out where a comma belongs is to read a sentence aloud and pay attention to where you pause or take a breath. Ask your child to do the same. Here are two more easy rules to keep in mind.

* **Use a comma to separate words or phrases in a list.** *(I need to buy milk, eggs, butter, and sugar today.)*

* **Use a comma between two or more adjectives that modify the same noun.** *(The large, yellow cat slept all day.)* Remember that no comma is needed between the final adjective and the noun itself.

Commas to separate words in a list, including two or more adjectives that modify the same noun

---

We did this in class!

Directions: Read each sentence and insert a comma to separate words in a list and between two or more adjectives that modify the same noun. HINT: Read these out loud and try putting the comma where you naturally pause in your reading.

1. I have four pencils an eraser three notebooks and a red folder inside my bag.

2. José Kathy and Marina are going to the playground after school.

3. Would you like to have a puppy a goldfish a lizard or a ferret?

4. The huge red balloon sailed over the playground.

5. The bulletin board had a large shiny poster on it.

Name _____ Date _____

I. Directions: Write complete sentences in response to the statements below. Be sure to place commas where they belong.

1. Name four things that are in your desk.

    _____

2. Name five kids in your class who do not wear glasses.

    _____

3. List four articles of clothing you wore to school today.

    _____

4. Use two or more adjectives to describe today's weather.

    _____

5. Use two or more adjectives to describe your best friend.

    _____

II. Directions: Read each sentence below aloud. Listen for the pause, which may indicate where a comma should go. Write "correct" if the commas are in their right places. Write "incorrect" if they are not.

_____   1. Our dogs are named Fido, Rover, and Spot.

_____   2. We waited on the fresh green grass.

_____   3. The sound of the loud, screaming siren was coming closer each minute

_____   4. The spacious, new, airplane was ready to take off.

· ·

This homework is due at school on _____ .

_____   _____
        Child's signature   Parent's signature

Dear Families,

This homework will focus on three simple rules for using commas.

* **Use a comma after a mild interjection or exclamation.** (*Wow, look at the time!*)

* **Use a comma after an introductory word or phrase at the beginning of a sentence.** (*After we wash the dishes, we can go to the movies.*)

* **Use a comma to set off the name of the person to whom you are speaking.** (*Talia, please don't tease the dog.*)

These may seem like very straightforward rules, but be careful! Sometimes the word or phrase that needs a comma is in the middle or at the end of the sentence. In this case, you need a comma before and after the word(s).

Please bring me a pencil, Susan, so I can write a grocery list.

To make this lesson easier, remind your child to read the sentences aloud to hear where he or she naturally pauses. This is usually where a comma should be inserted.

Commas after an interjection or an introductory phrase, and to set off a person's name when addressing that person

We did this in class!

Directions: After each sentence, please indicate where the comma should be inserted.

Example: *So do you want the red or the green hat?*
(Put comma after *So*.)

1. Whenever we go to Grandma's house she makes us chocolate chip cookies.

_____

2. Well where do you think we should go for lunch? _____

3. Would you please let the cat out Pam? _____

4. After we finish lunch we'll go to the playground. _____

5. Close the door Jake so the cat won't get out. _____

Name _____ Date _____

Families, please help!

I. Directions: Use a red pencil or marker to add at least one big comma to each sentence.

1. Sam what are you talking about?

2. Okay I will see you in about an hour.

3. Lourdes may I see you after school?

4. When we get to the pool I will have to buy season passes.

5. Where would you like to go on vacation Luis?

6. Yes we have some orange juice in the refrigerator.

II. Directions: Use a red pencil or marker to put big commas where they belong in these sentences. HINT: Some sentences do not need a comma, while others may need two commas.

1. Tim did you see that big fish?

2. Yes I saw it Joey but that was not a fish.

3. Not a fish? What was it?

4. I think it was a turtle.

5. It couldn't be a turtle Tim. Turtles have shells you know.

6. Yes I know. That is why I think it was a turtle. It had a shell Joey.

7. Okay Tim. You must be right. Maybe it wasn't a fish.

8. Maybe it was a shellfish!

· ·

This homework is due at school on _____ .

_____   _____
         Child's signature   Parent's signature

Dear Families,

One way to help children understand where commas go is to have them read sentences aloud and note where they pause or take a breath. Punctuation marks act like traffic signals. So, if the period is like a red light (telling us to stop), then a comma is like a yellow light that signals us to slow down or pause. Here are two more rules about commas.

❋ **Use a comma to set off appositives, or descriptive phrases.** *(Sally, our babysitter, broke her leg.)*

An *appositive* is a word or phrase that comes right after another word, defining or describing that word. In the above example, *Sally* is *our babysitter*, so we can use the phrases interchangeably. An appositive can be at the beginning, middle, or end of a sentence.

Our babysitter, Sally, broke her leg.

The girl with the broken leg is our babysitter, Sally.

❋ **Use commas to set off words that are not essential to the meaning of the sentence.** *(Mr. Jones, of course, was not at the meeting.)* The essence of the sentence is that Mr. Jones was not at the meeting.

Some sentences contain words or phrases, such as *however, naturally,* or *of course,* that interrupt the flow of the sentence and are not critical to the meaning. Use commas to set off these nonessential words or phrases.

Commas to set off appositives and words that are not essential to the meaning of a sentence

---

We did this in class!

Directions: Use a red crayon, marker, or pencil to make big commas where they belong in these sentences. HINT: Read these aloud and put the comma where you naturally pause.

1. Mrs. Smith who is our teacher has decided to retire.

2. We were sad when our favorite teacher Mrs. Smith decided to retire.

3. We loved the book by Mr. Morris who used to write for the newspaper.

4. Ivania of course was never late for school.

5. It was the music teacher naturally who played the piano at the talent show.

Name _____ Date _____

Families, please help!

I. Directions: Read each sentence aloud and listen for the pause to help you decide where a comma should go. Use a red pencil or marker to insert commas. HINT: One sentence does not need a comma at all!

1. Every child obviously wanted to be first in line.

2. The leaves were all orange and yellow naturally as it was October.

3. The crowd waited for hours in the hot sun.

4. What should I do then with the old books?

5. Joey got first prize surprisingly even though his costume was homemade.

II. Directions: Use a red marker or pencil to put big commas where they belong in the paragraphs. HINT: Not every sentence needs a comma, but some may need two.

One day our teacher Mr. Conner said we were going to do a special project. We would be working with clay one of the oldest materials used in art.

Mr. Conner showed us how to pat the clay and smooth it with the side of a glass. To make circles we used cutters that looked like my mom's old metal biscuit cutter. Next he told us to roll the clay into a ribbon which looked like a snake. We put the ribbon around the edge of the clay circle and wrapped it around and around sort of like a Slinky toy.

Next Mr. Conner who was so patient showed us how to wet our fingers and smooth the clay to make the sides of the pot. The pots were nearly finished. Finally Mr. Conner baked them in a special oven also known as a kiln.

This homework is due at school on _____ .

_____   _____
Child's signature   Parent's signature

Comma Lesson #4

Week-by-Week Homework for Building Grammar, Usage, and Mechanics Skills © 2010 by Mary Rose, Scholastic Teaching Resources

Dear Families,

You may be aware that the comma is one of the most misused punctuation marks. Even adults are rarely sure where commas should and should not go. Today's homework is one of the most straightforward lessons about punctuation, so you can rest easy!

* **Use a comma after the greeting in a friendly letter.**
  (Dear Janice,)

* **Use a comma in the closing of a friendly letter.**
  (Sincerely, Doug)

Commas to punctuate the greeting and closing in a friendly letter

....

We did this in class!

Directions: Write a response to this letter.

Dear Student,

What is your most difficult subject in school? The Homework Helper Hotline is working hard to give you homework help. We need to know what subjects are toughest for you, so we can prepare to help. Your reply is appreciated.

Best wishes,
Homework Helper

_____

_____

_____

_____

_____

Name _____   Date _____

Directions: Read the letters below. Use a red pencil or marker to add commas where they belong.

Dear Homework Helper

   My name is Barbara. I really need your help with a math concept. What does my teacher mean when she talks about a square root? The only roots I know are underground.

Signed
Baffled Barbara

Dear Baffled Barbara

   Thank you so much for contacting the Homework Helper. Do you know how to multiply? Can you multiply a number by itself, like 3x3? Well, the answer you get is 9; the square root of 9 is 3. The square root is the number you multiplied by itself to get that larger number. Does this help?

Sincerely
Homework Helper

Dear Homework Helper

   Yes, it does help. Tell me if I have these correct: The square root of 16 is 4, since I multiply 4x4 to get it. The square root of 36 is 6. Am I on the right track?

Yours truly
Unbaffled Barbara

Dear Unbaffled Barbara

   You've got it! Thanks for contacting Homework Helper. Please write again soon.

Your ever-faithful friend
Homework Helper

This homework is due at school on _____ .

_____   _____
            Child's signature   Parent's signature

Comma Lesson #5

Name _____ Date _____

Directions: Please use a red marker or pencil to add commas where they belong in these letters.

Dear Mr. Waltz

I have not seen you since May 25 2005. I read an article by Alexis Burling an editor for *Storyworks* magazine. It was published on April 1 2007 and was called "The Music Man." Here's what I learned.

Well about 1,000 years ago there was no way to write musical notes on paper. People could not of course share music unless they could remember exactly how it was supposed to sound. This was very difficult for most people.

A young intelligent monk named Guido lived in Arezzo Italy. Guido could play the harp guitar and lute. The young monk looked at his hand and got an idea. He saw lines and spaces and called this a "staff." Finally he wrote a song and added words from a poem.

Mr. Waltz I hope you're enjoying retirement from being band director.

Your former student

Neil

Dear Former Student

Neil I am proud of you for learning about how music was first written. I have heard of Guido the inventor of written music. We still use his invention today. He also invented the notes and what they look like.

I moved to Lexington Nebraska on August 17 2005. I am enjoying retirement because I get to cook garden and walk my dogs. I think of you as one of my favorite students and wonder what you're up to now. Wow I can see you're still the bright boy I remember.

Musically yours

Mr. Waltz

Apostrophes: Contractions & Possessives

We use apostrophes to form contractions and possessives. "To contract" means to shorten, and a *contraction* is when two words are "shortened" into one. Contractions can speed up our speaking and make it seem more natural. We use contractions on a daily basis, but they should not be used in business letters, formal essays, reports, etc.

To make a contraction, we omit one or more letters from two words and replace the letters with an apostrophe. Put the apostrophe in the exact place of the omitted letter(s). Common contractions include: *I'll, I'm, don't, doesn't, can't, he's, she's, it's, there's, they're, we're, you're.*

We also use apostrophes to form possessives—words that show ownership. We generally form a possessive by adding an apostrophe and an *s* (**'s**): *the girl's book.* For plural words ending in *s*, we usually add the apostrophe after the *s* (**s'**): *both girls' books.*

Overview of the Skills

Tip

Write *will not* on the board and see if children figure out that the contraction is *won't*, not *willn't*. Another tricky contraction is *can't*; it is a shortened form of *cannot*, which is already one word.

Tip

Teach students that *it's* is a contraction for *it is*. This is often confused with the possessive *its*. Reinforce this when covering possessives. Another contraction to note is *let's*. Make sure students know it stands for *let us* (not *let is*).

Lesson #1

Negative contractions—contractions that combine a verb and the word *not*

Contractions are often "negative contractions," meaning one of the shortened words is *not*. To make a negative contraction, we simply take out the letter *o* from *not*, replace it with an apostrophe, and merge the two words into one. Make sure students grasp this concept: *does not, doesn't; do not, don't; did not, didn't; is not, isn't; has not, hasn't; would not, wouldn't*; and so on.

Lesson #2

Contractions that combine a pronoun and a verb

Some contractions combine a pronoun and a verb. Your students may not know what a "pronoun" is, but they use them all the time, and these contractions will be familiar. A pronoun takes the place of a noun. Pronouns include: *you, I, he, she, it, we,* and *they*. Some verbs used in contractions include: *am, is, are, have, will*. Students will recognize these examples as you write them on the board and read them aloud: *I'm, we're, they're, she's, you'll, I've, you've*, etc. Remind students that we place the apostrophe exactly where letters have been omitted.

Lesson #3

Unconventional contractions

The contractions in this lesson are sometimes difficult to read and to pronounce. They are presented here because students often encounter them in literature, usually in dialogue, and they may need to know how to write them if they are attempting to write dialogue. We call them "unconventional" because they are often clumsy and are rarely used in formal writing. These can also be difficult to spell because the apostrophe can sometimes represent several missing letters. *Remind students to place the apostrophe where letters have been omitted.* Emphasize that these contractions should not be used in formal writing, unless they are in a direct quotation. Examples include: *would've, could've, should've, who'd, you'd, he'd, they'd.* (Note that these can be confusing; *he'd* might be *he had* or *he would*.)

Lesson #4

Apostrophes to denote possession

This lesson is, perhaps, the most difficult of all apostrophe lessons. That's because the possessive apostrophe in "Fred's computer is broken," looks just like the contraction apostrophe in "Fred's coming to dinner" (a contraction of *Fred is*). Students can get confused and then either put the apostrophe in the wrong place or simply leave it out. However, the most common mistake with apostrophes is when it comes to plural possessives:

 * *All the dogs have blue collars. The dogs' collars are blue.*

 Provide students with many examples that show plural nouns ending in *s* and work with them in adding an apostrophe after the *s* to show possession. Eventually, you can discuss plural possessives that do not end in s: *children, children's; people, people's*; etc.

Lesson #5

Avoiding double negatives with contractions

Fortunately, many of you can skip this lesson. Double negatives do pop up from time to time: *We haven't got no soup today; She hasn't got nobody to play with.* Sometimes when creating a negative contraction, a student will forget to check that there are no other negative words (*no, none, nobody*, etc.) left in the sentence. However, unless your students are making these kinds of errors, don't do this lesson, as it may only confuse them.

Tip

 * Review the rules for making plurals (adding -s or -es). Remind students that "**'s**" is used for possessives, not to make a singular noun plural.

 * Take this opportunity to reinforce an exception: *its*. This possessive does not have an apostrophe so it won't be confused with "it is" (*it's*).

Name _____ Date _____

I. Directions: Read each contraction. Then write the two words from which it was made.

Example: they'll   they will

1. you'll   _____

2. don't   _____

3. that's   _____

4. I've   _____

5. won't   _____

6. Susan's   _____

7. couldn't   _____

8. it's   _____

II. Directions: Read the following words and then write them as contractions.

Example: we were   we're

1. is not   _____

2. have not   _____

3. he is   _____

4. they are   _____

5. are not   _____

6. would not _____

7. there is   _____

8. I would   _____

III. Directions: Read the following phrases and write them as possessives using an apostrophe.

Example: the bike belongs to Jim   Jim's bike

1. the cake belongs to Sue   _____

2. Jill owns the pail   _____

3. Doug owns red pants   _____

4. the toys belong to the cats _____

5. the house of my aunt   _____

Week-by-Week Homework for Building Grammar, Usage, and Mechanics Skills © 2010 by Mary Rose, Scholastic Teaching Strategies

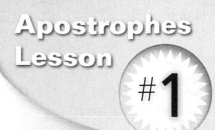

Dear Families,

Although contractions should not be used in research papers, reports, formal letters, or essays, we do want our students to understand them. A *contraction* is a shortening of two words into one. We omit one or more letters and replace them with an apostrophe (**'**). It is important that the words are merged into one and that the apostrophe is placed exactly where the letters are missing. This lesson deals with "negative contractions."

Negative contractions— contractions that combine a verb and the word *not*

❋ **A negative contraction combines a verb and *not*. It merges the two words using an apostrophe.** (*are not, aren't; is not, isn't; had not, hadn't,* etc.)

You can help your child do well on these assignments by making sure he or she understands that the placement of the apostrophe is critical. It is also important that your child recognizes which letters have been omitted.

....

We did this in class!

Directions: Rewrite the words in parentheses as a contraction. HINT: Notice that *can't* is an exception to the rule, as it began as one word, *cannot*.

1. Steve (is not) _____ going home early today.

2. We (cannot) _____ wait until summer vacation.

3. We (were not) _____ late for school today.

4. You (should not) _____ run in the hallway of school.

5. Lakeisha (will not) _____ finish her work before lunch. (Tricky!)

Name _____ Date _____

Directions: Rewrite the words in parentheses as a contraction.

Our school is having a fundraiser this fall. We (will not) _____ have any

trouble selling candy to make money for our school. I (have not) _____ seen

the prizes yet, but they are always great. They (do not) _____ give a prize to

everyone who sells, but they usually give one to the top seller in each classroom. Last year, they

gave it to both a boy and a girl. I (do not) _____ remember the boy who got

it last year, but it (was not) _____ me. I (did not) _____

try very hard because I was too busy playing baseball after school. Margie won the girl's

prize in our class. If it (had not) _____ been for her, the rest of us would

have had a chance. Her mom and dad helped her sell the candy where they work. That (is not)

_____ fair, and it makes it hard for the rest of us.

    They also give a prize to the student who sells the most in the whole school. I (could not)

_____ believe it when I saw what the prize was last year: a new trick bicycle.

That was a prize any kid would love.

    They have already passed out the permission slips that our parents have to sign so we can

start selling. I (cannot) _____ wait to get the candy, since I usually eat some

on my way home from school. It (does not) _____ seem to matter if I like it

or not—I just have to eat some while I am carrying it. It is amazing that I have any left to sell!

. . . .

This homework is due at school on _____ .

_____   _____
         Child's signature   Parent's signature

Dear Families,

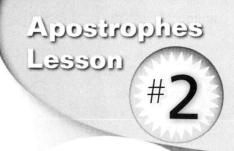

Contractions that combine a pronoun and a verb

Although contractions should not be used in research papers, reports, formal letters, or essays, we do want our students to understand them. A contraction is a shortening of two words into one. We simply omit one or more letters and replace them with an apostrophe ('). It is important that the apostrophe be placed exactly where the letters are missing. Then, the two words are merged into one.

There are several kinds of contractions. This lesson deals with those that combine a pronoun (e.g., *I, you, he, she, we, they*) and a verb or helping verb (e.g., *am, is, are, will,* etc.).

❋ **A contraction can combine a pronoun and a verb using an apostrophe.**

For example, *you will* becomes *you'll*; *they are* becomes *they're*; and *who is* becomes *who's*.

Help your child understand that sometimes a contraction omits one letter and sometimes it omits more than one.

....

We did this in class!

Directions: Rewrite the words in parentheses as a contraction.

1. (You have) _____ just won first prize in the raffle!

2. (It is) _____ time for you to get ready for bed.

3. (We have) _____ all had a chance to take the pet mouse home for the weekend.

4. (Let us) _____ get to work on our math now. (Hint: Tricky!)

5. (They are) _____ almost finished painting the hallway.

6. I am sure (they will) _____ win the soccer match tonight.

Name _____ Date _____

Families, please help!

I. Directions: Rewrite the words in parentheses as a contraction.

1. (I will) _____ help you with your homework.

2. (You are) _____ welcome to join us at this table.

3. (He is) _____ sure to do well on the essay today.

4. (You have) _____ scored the most points of anyone in the game.

5. (Who is) _____ in charge of the lunch money?

6. (We are) _____ not going on a field trip this month.

II. Directions: Rewrite the contraction as the two words from which it was made.

1. (She'll) _____ definitely win the art contest.

2. (They've) _____ always been generous people.

3. (They'll) _____ get it right next time.

4. (It'll) _____ be winter soon.

5. I am sure (we'll) _____ finish our math by 3:00.

6. (Let's) _____ try to keep a positive attitude this year.

This homework is due at school on _____ .

_____   _____
           Child's signature   Parent's signature

Dear Families,

Certain types of contractions are considered unconventional and are mostly used in conversation and in casual literature. These contractions are used in everyday language when we speak to one another, but they should not be used when speaking or writing in formal situations, such as essays, reports, or speeches.

* **Unconventional contractions often combine a pronoun with *could*, *would*, *should*, or *had*. As with other contractions, put an apostrophe where letters have been omitted.**

Examples of unconventional contractions are: *I'd*, *who'd*, and *they'd*. (Note that these can be confusing: *I'd* could mean *I had* or *I would*, which is another reason they should not be used in formal writing.) Because elementary students do not often see these words in print, they have trouble spelling them. This lesson will help students with these words.

We did this in class!

Directions: Match the two words in the first column to the contraction in the second column.

1.	you would		I'd
2.	I would		we'd
3.	she would		you'd
4.	could have		that'd
5.	we would		could've
6.	that would		she'd
7.	I had		I'd
8.	we had		should've
9.	it had		we'd
10.	should have		it'd

Name _____ Date _____

Directions: Read the following story. In the spaces following the words in bold type, write a contraction for those two words. Refer to the list on the previous page for help.

Record-Breaking Folks

Have you ever heard of *The Guinness Book of World Records*? **I had** _____

heard of it before, but never bothered reading it. Well, things have changed. Now, I love

checking out this book each year. **You would** _____ be amazed by the stories,

facts, and pictures in that book! There are things **that will** _____ shock and

astound you. There is a story about a woman who collects different kinds of rubber ducks—

1,439 of them. **She would** _____ surely have enough to fill her bathtub! There is

an article about the man with the biggest feet—size 29! Now, **he would** _____

have trouble shoe shopping at Wal-Mart! **Who would** _____ have guessed that

The Guinness Book of World Records would become one of the best-selling books of all time?

If **you have** _____ ever wanted to get your name in the book, you need a

special trick. **It had** _____ best be something no one else has tried before.

It needs to be a skill or feat **that will** _____ impress the editors. I am sure

the editors thought **they had** _____ heard of everything until they met Kym

Coberly. She is a woman **you have** _____ probably heard of. She can hula-hoop

with 99 hula hoops at one time. **That would** _____ take some practice!

Well, **I had** _____ best be going. Time to see who has balanced 40 glasses on

his chin (Ashrita Furman).

....

This homework is due at school on _____ .

_____   _____
Child's signature   Parent's signature

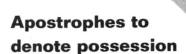

Apostrophes to denote possession

Dear Families,

By far the most confusing use of the apostrophe is to show ownership (*Julie's dog*). Because it looks the same as a contraction that contains *is* (*Julie's going home now*, meaning Julie *is* going home now), students (and adults) are easily confused. Most people do not get confused when they are reading, but have difficulty when writing. And because there is an s involved, it can be more confusing when it comes to plurals. These rules should help.

* **For singular possessives, add an apostrophe and an *s* ('s): *Jan's car***

* **For plural words ending in *s*, add the apostrophe after the *s* (s'): the *boys' bikes***

* **For plurals that don't end in *s*, add an apostrophe and *s* ('s): the *children's toys***

Note that the apostrophe can also be used with nouns that are not names. (*The forest's beauty is breathtaking.*) Remember that we do NOT use the apostrophe when we simply mean to make a word plural. (*The world has few untouched forests.*)

....

We did this in class!

Directions: In each sentence, you'll find a word with an apostrophe. If the apostrophe is used in a contraction, write *contraction* on the line provided. If the apostrophe is used to show possession, write *possession* on the line.

1. That is the school's book. _____

2. We went over to Maria's house. _____

3. Jenna's the most talented writer in the class. _____

4. Our class thinks he's the best singer. _____

5. Juan's baseball glove was stolen. _____

6. Barbara's already gone home. _____

Name _____ Date _____

Families, please help!

I. Directions: In each sentence below you will find a name with an apostrophe. If this is a contraction (a combination of two words), write *contraction* on the line. If the apostrophe shows ownership or possession, write *possession*.

1. Frank's always hungry. _____

2. Claire's car is new. _____

3. Joyce's cat has fleas. _____

4. Bill's trophy is broken. _____

5. Piedmont's reading scores are always the highest in the county. _____

6. Piedmont's working hard to improve their math scores. _____

II. Directions: In these examples, there are no names, but the directions are the same as above. Write the word *contraction* or *possession* after each sentence.

1. She's really good at sewing. _____

2. The dog's tail was wagging. _____

3. The car's tire was flat. _____

4. The school's lights were not on. _____

5. School's out for the summer. _____

6. It's raining outside. _____

· ·

This homework is due at school on _____ .

_____   _____
         Child's signature   Parent's signature

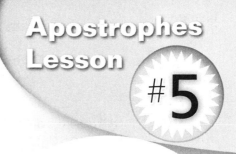

Dear Families,

When students use contractions, they often fall into the trap of creating a double negative—a sentence that has two negative words. (*She hasn't got no money.* Both *hasn't* and *no* are negative words.) There should be only one negative word in a sentence. (*She has* no *money;* or *She* hasn't *got any money.*)

It is easy to spot a negative word, because they usually begin with the letter *n*. Examples include *no, not, nobody, nothing, nowhere, none, never, no one, nor,* and *neither.* Although they don't begin with the letter *n*, the words *hardly, scarcely,* and *barely* are also considered negative words.

The best way to correct a double negative is to change one negative word into a positive. You can either take it out or drop the *-n't* at the end of a word. (See example above.)

Avoiding double negatives with negative contractions

We did this in class!

Directions: Read each sentence below and circle both negative words. Then rewrite each of these sentences two different ways so that each contains only one negative word. Circle the one negative word in each sentence you create.

1. They haven't got no mail this morning.

   _____

   _____

2. Bill isn't going nowhere today.

   _____

   _____

3. Sheila hasn't nobody to talk to.

   _____

   _____

4. There isn't nothing you can do about the weather.

   _____

   _____

Name _____ Date _____

Families, please help!

Directions: The sentences below are incorrect because they contain two negative words (called a "double negative"). Please read each sentence aloud and circle both negative words. Then rewrite the sentences two different ways so that they contain only one negative word. Circle the one negative word in each of the sentences you create.

1. That dog hasn't never barked at a stranger.

   _____

   _____

2. I haven't got none left.

   _____

   _____

3. There isn't no one at home today.

   _____

   _____

4. I don't hardly have any time these days.

   _____

   _____

5. They don't have nothing to wear to the party.

   _____

   _____

· ·

This homework is due at school on _____ .

_____   _____
          Child's signature   Parent's signature

Name _____ Date _____

I. Directions: Read each contraction. Then write the two words from which they were made.

Example: they'll   <u>they will</u>

1. that's _____

2. they'd _____

3. she's _____

4. you've _____

5. it'll _____

6. who's _____

7. you've _____

8. mustn't _____

9. Linda's _____

10. didn't _____

II. Directions: Read the following phrases, then rewrite them as contractions or possessives.

Examples: we were   <u>we're</u>
            Jane owns the car   <u>Jane's car</u>

1. the toy belongs to the baby _____

2. will not _____

3. we would _____

4. did not _____

5. essays of the students _____

6. what is _____

7. he will _____

8. they have _____

9. Markeshia is _____

10. we have _____

Quotations & Quotation Marks

Figuring out when and where to use quotation marks can cause great consternation for both children and adults. Students may wonder why one title is in quotation marks, when another is in italics. And where do quotation marks go when writing dialogue or quoting someone? Because students do not know how to punctuate dialogue, teachers sometimes discourage them from using it in their stories.

Many of the issues about quotations, quotation marks, and punctuation are addressed here. Let's start with something basic: using quotation marks when there is *no* dialogue involved.

Overview of the Skills

Lesson # 1

Use quotation marks around the titles of songs, poems, short stories, chapters, essays, and newspaper and magazine articles.

As if writing weren't complicated enough, we actually use quotation marks around words that are NOT a direct quote. The simplest way to teach this is to go over numerous examples. Then, make a list and post it on a bulletin board. Be sure your examples follow this pattern:

"The Boy Who Lived"—a chapter (in *Harry Potter and the Sorcerer's Stone*)
"The Gift of the Magi"—a short story (O. Henry)
"The Killer Fungus"—an article (in *Time* magazine)
"Life Is a Highway"—a song (Rascal Flatts)
"Song of Myself"—a poem (Walt Whitman)

Lesson #2

Use quotation marks around the exact words of the speaker. Capitalize the first word of the quotation. Set apart the "tag line" (which identifies the speaker) with a comma.

This lesson contains simple quotes with no fancy breaks or tricky issues. Give students practice by having them read from any book that contains dialogue. You might have them read the actual dialogue aloud and leave the narration to silent reading. You can also let pairs read aloud together: One child reads the dialogue, and the other reads the narration.

Here's a simple model lesson for teaching about dialogue punctuation:

* *Let's go to the park said Morgan.*

What are the exact words that Morgan said? _____
Make sure the first word is capitalized.

Put quotation marks where she starts talking and where she stops.
Insert a comma to set apart the tag line. (The tag line is *said Morgan*.)
In this case, the comma goes inside the quotation marks.

Tip

To make the most of
your teaching time,
you may want to do
this lesson during
Literature Circle
time, Reading or
Writing Center time,
or with guided-
reading groups.

Lesson #3

When a sentence in a quote is broken into two parts, do not capitalize the first word in the second part. Use commas before and after the tag line. Put end punctuation inside the quotation marks.

Display examples, like those below, of quotes that are broken into parts. Be sure to point out that, although separated, the second part of the quotation is a continuation of the same sentence, and thus does not begin with a capital letter.

* *"My brother Jim," Sam boasted, "is captain of the football team."*
* *"My sister," said Jane, "is captain of the soccer team, and they're in 1st place!"*

To show the importance of tag lines and how to punctuate them, choose a book with dialogue. Read portions aloud, but omit the tag lines (*said Bill* or *explained Mother*, for example). Students will find that the story doesn't make sense because they can't tell who is speaking.

Continue with examples that feature sections of dialogue with two or more speakers. First, display a sample with all the tag lines deleted or blacked out. Have volunteers read the selection (or try to). Discuss how confusing it is without knowing who is speaking. Next, display the sample with the tag lines and punctuation in place. It should make sense now.

Use the same selections to highlight the placement of end punctuation.

Lesson #4

If a quote has two or more sentences, start each sentence with a capital letter. End punctuation goes inside the quotation marks.

Students need practice with dialogue and placement of end punctuation. Do activities similar to those for Lesson 3, but use examples that feature dialogue or quotations with two or more sentences. Be sure students know to start each sentence with a capital letter.

Lesson #5

When writing dialogue, each new speaker gets a new paragraph.

Often, when students write dialogue, they put whole conversations in one long paragraph. Here's a fix: Have students make a new paragraph for each speaker, and put narration into a separate paragraph, too.

To teach the importance of structuring dialogue with paragraph breaks for different speakers, show students an example without these breaks. They will certainly have trouble making sense of the passage. Then, show students the same selection with the dialogue paragraphing included. Discuss how much clearer it is. Create practice exercises in which students insert paragraph breaks.

Name _____ Date _____

I. Directions: Read the following sentences. Put quotation marks where you think they belong. HINT: Some sentences do NOT need any. Capitalize if necessary, too.

1. One of my favorite movies is *The Chronicles of Narnia*.

2. Do you know all of the words to The Itsy, Bitsy Spider?

3. Have you ever read *The Cat in the Hat*, by Dr. Seuss?

4. When I went through the door, I heard everyone say, Happy Birthday!

5. When I grow up, said Alma, I want to be a scientist.

6. Sabrina said, when I grow up, I want to be a nurse. I want to help sick children.

II. Directions: Read the following sentences. Put commas and quotation marks where they belong.

1. I want a pony for my birthday said Kathryn.

2. I don't want a pony said William. I want a dog.

3. Why would you want a dog? asked Kathryn. You can't ride a dog.

4. I want a dog because I can sleep with him. You can't sleep with a pony explained William.

Dear Families,

Of all of the punctuation skills in the English language, none is more puzzling to students than the use of quotation marks. Here are some rules for using quotation marks that are NOT related to writing dialogue or quoting someone.

* **Use quotation marks around the titles of songs, poems, short stories, chapters, essays, and articles in newspapers and magazines. (We underline or italicize the titles of books and movies.)**

Quotation marks around the titles of songs, poems, short stories, plays, chapters, essays, and newspaper and magazine articles

---

We did this in class!

Directions: Read the paragraph below and insert quotation marks where necessary.

Our Reading Class

Our reading teacher made us read all kinds of stuff, not just stories from our reading books. This year, our favorite book was *Harry Potter and the Sorcerer's Stone.* We all knew it was going to be a great book because the first chapter was called The Boy Who Lived. It was great to read this with friends.

We also had poetry folders this year. Each Friday, our teacher gave us pages of poetry to keep in them, and we didn't even have to do any work pages with them. We just read the poetry for fun. My favorite poem was Tattooin' Ruth, by Shel Silverstein.

Another favorite thing we read this year was *Storyworks* magazine. It comes out six times a year and has poetry, fiction, nonfiction, and a play in each issue. Our whole class loved The Tell-Tale Heart, by Edgar Allen Poe, and we enjoyed acting out The Adventure of the Red-Headed League, a story by Sir Arthur Conan Doyle.

Name _____   Date _____

Directions: Read the paragraph below and put quotation marks around the titles of songs, poems, short stories, chapter or essay titles, and titles of newspaper and magazine articles.

What did you read over summer vacation? I tried to read all kinds of things—books, plays, short stories. I even read the back of cereal boxes! It is amazing how much riboflavin is in cereal!

The best books I read were ten of the old Nancy Drew books by Carolyn Keene. I had to laugh when I saw a chapter called The Mysterious Black Cat because I have one of those at my house.

I also read a lot of poetry. Have you ever heard of a poet named David Harrison? He writes really interesting poems, like I Waited Too Long. I also like Jack Prelutsky because he writes about holidays. I Ate Too Much is a really funny poem about Thanksgiving.

My mom bought me some magazines to read over the summer, too. My favorite is *American Girl*. This year, it had a story called The New Kid. I enjoyed it because I will be the new kid when school starts in September.

So, what did I do when I WASN'T reading? I listened to music, of course. I just discovered Josh Groban and his beautiful song, You Raise Me Up.

- -

This homework is due at school on _____ .

_____   _____
Child's signature   Parent's signature

Dear Families,

There are about 12 rules for writing direct quotations and dialogue, but we will focus on only the three most basic rules. They include rules for capitalization and commas.

* **Put beginning and ending quotation marks around the exact words of the speaker.** (*"Jim wants to go to the lake."*)

* **Capitalize the first word of the quotation.** (*Trevor said, "Jim wants to go to the lake."*)

* **Set apart the tag line with a comma.** The *tag line* tells who the speaker is. (In the example above, *Trevor said* is the tag line.)

Quotation marks around the exact words of the speaker; capitalization and punctuation of direct quotes and "tag lines"

We did this in class!

Directions: Follow the rules above and the instructions below to punctuate these sentences. Circle the first letter of each phrase that is the direct quote. HINT: The "direct quote" means these are exactly the words the person said.

It is time for lunch said Mrs. Baker.

What are the exact words that Mrs. Baker said? _____

Put quotation marks where she starts talking. Now, put them where she stops talking.

Insert a comma to separate the tag line. (The tag line is *said Mrs. Baker.*)

The children said we are hungry.

What are the exact words that the children said? _____

Put quotation marks where they start talking. Put them where they stop talking.

Capitalize the first word the speaker says.

Insert a comma to separate the tag line. (The tag line is *The children said.*)

Name _____ Date _____

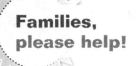

Families, please help!

Directions: Follow the directions below to punctuate these sentences.

For each sentence, say to yourself, "What are the exact words that were said by Mother, Father, and Luis?" (HINT: The sentence you just read is a model for you to use.) Circle the capital letter that starts their words; this is the start of the direct quote. Put quotation marks where each one started talking. Put quotation marks where each stopped talking. Insert commas as needed to set apart the tag lines. HINT: One sentence does not need quotation marks. If a quote already has punctuation, like a question mark or exclamation point, before the tag line, you do not need to add a comma.

Luis said I really want a puppy.

Mother said You cannot have a dog.

Luis said Maurice has puppies for sale.

Mother said I know Maurice has puppies for sale.

They are only twenty-five dollars said Luis.

Do you have twenty-five dollars? asked Mother.

No, I don't have twenty-five dollars said Luis.

Then how will you buy a puppy? asked Mother.

Luis smiled and said I thought you would buy one for me.

Mother smiled back and said You thought wrong, Luis.

Then Father was standing in the doorway.

Maybe Father will buy a puppy for me said Luis.

You won't get a puppy if your mother says no said Father.

May I get one if I save my own money? asked Luis.

Father and Mother said Twenty-five dollars is a lot of money. We'll see.

· ·

This homework is due at school on _____ .

_____   _____
Child's signature   Parent's signature

Week-by-Week Homework for Building Grammar, Usage, and Mechanics Skills © 2010 by Mary Rose, Scholastic Teaching Resources

Dear Families,

Writing dialogue and using direct quotations is often difficult, and sometimes the format of our speech further complicates and confuses students. This is true when quotations are broken apart. Here are two examples and some rules to guide you.

"I think," said Maria, "that a storm is coming."

"Mom," asked Terry, "is the kitchen window still open?"

* **If the quotation is broken into two parts, do not capitalize the first word in the second part of the quotation.** (It is a continuation of the same sentence.)

* **Put a comma before the tag line and after the tag line.**

* **Put end punctuation inside the final quotation mark.**

Quotations in two parts: capitalization and punctuation; putting end punctuation inside quotation marks

. . . .

We did this in class!

Directions: Rewrite each sentence and add quotation marks around the exact words that are spoken. Be sure to include commas before and after each tag line. Remember: The end punctuation (exclamation point, period, question mark) goes inside the quotation marks.

1. I think said Mrs. Rodriguez that we should have a special reading class today.

   _____

2. What asked the children will we do differently?

   _____

3. Well explained the teacher we will have our reading class under the big oak tree.

   _____

4. Hurrah! Mrs. Rodriguez cheered the children you are the best!

   _____

Name _____ Date _____

Directions: Rewrite each sentence and put quotation marks around the exact words that are spoken. Be sure to include commas before and after each tag line. Look on the front of this paper for rules and examples. HINT: End punctuation (exclamation point, period, question mark) goes *inside* the quotation marks.

1. Today is a good day Mrs. Chiu explained for getting a class pet.

   _____

2. Yes shouted the children that would be a great idea!

   _____

3. Well asked Mrs. Chiu what pet do you think we should get?

   _____

4. I think answered Jerry we should get mice.

   _____

5. Okay agreed Mrs. Chiu mice will be the perfect pets for our classroom.

   _____

. . . .

This homework is due at school on _____ .

_____   _____
        Child's signature   Parent's signature

Dear Families,

Almost every student struggles when learning where to place quotation marks. The rules are really quite simple, but the way we speak and write can make it confusing. Everything that is a direct quote (a person's exact words) needs to be inside quotation marks. Sometimes this is only one sentence; sometimes it is a whole paragraph. Here are some basic rules:

Quotations with separate sentences: capitalization and punctuation

* **If the quotation has two separate sentences, they both start with a capital letter.**

* **End punctuation belongs inside the quotation marks.**

We did this in class!

Directions: Read the following story and add quotation marks around the exact words that someone said. For this exercise, quotation marks are the only punctuation you need to add.

Mrs. Sanders said, You are not going to believe where we are going on our field trip.

You are going to love this!

Where, where, where? asked every child in the class.

I'm not going to tell you, replied Mrs. Sanders. I'm going to see if you can guess.

Give us a hint, begged the children. Give us a big, big hint.

We are staying in Orlando, explained Mrs. Sanders. We are going to EPCOT.

We're going to Disney World! shouted the children.

We are, said Mrs. Sanders. Disney is letting all fourth graders in Florida visit free.

We even get a free lunch.

We can't wait! yelled the children. Disney World is the happiest place on Earth!

Name _____ Date _____

Families, please help!

Directions: Correctly punctuate the following paragraph with quotation marks and commas. (HINT: We use commas with tag lines.) In the last sentence, you will see an example of a time we use single quotation marks. Just remember, the ending quotation marks that you are adding go at the end of the entire quotation.

Who is the greatest NASCAR driver of all time? asked Jordan. Do you have a clue?

I don't know, I replied. Could it be Jeff Gordon?

No, said Jordan. It is Richard Petty.

I have heard of him, I said. What makes him so great?

You don't know? exclaimed Jordan. Do you live in a cave? How many wins does Jeff

Gordon have?

Jeff Gordon has 92 wins, almost a record, I bragged.

Well, if it is ALMOST a record, who holds the record for all-time NASCAR wins? Do you have

a clue now?

I don't know, I stammered. I guess the answer might be Richard Petty. How many wins does

he have?

Are you ready for this? asked Jordan. Richard Petty has 200 wins. What do you think of that?

I think that is pretty impressive, I said. Boy, I know why they always refer to him as 'The King.'

· ·

This homework is due at school on _____ .

_____   _____
Child's signature   Parent's signature

Week-by-Week Homework for Building Grammar, Usage, and Mechanics Skills © 2010 by Mary Rose, Scholastic Teaching Resources

Dear Families,

Teachers often discourage students from writing dialogue because it is so difficult to do. Students usually do not know where and how to use the punctuation (quotation marks, commas, question marks, and exclamation marks) that will make the "talk" make sense. Another thing students forget to do is to start a new paragraph each time a new person speaks. That's what we're working on here. This homework features a brief story that contains narration and conversation. Your child should indicate where to make a new paragraph. Here are some things to keep in mind:

* **When writing conversation, each new speaker gets a new paragraph.**

* **When quoting thoughts that are exact words, also use quotation marks and separate paragraphs.**

* **Start a new paragraph when the story switches to narration.** (Note: Professional writers are adept at mixing narration with conversation, but for students, it is easier to keep these separate.)

Writing dialogue: each new speaker gets a new paragraph

We did this in class!

Directions: The following story has been written as one long paragraph. Read the story and put a capital **P** everywhere that a new paragraph should start. HINT: There will be five paragraphs.

"Did you ever hear of the Little League World Series?" asked Lee. "It is held each summer in Cooperstown, New York." "Why do they hold it clear up there?" asked Isabelle. "They do it there because that is the location of the Baseball Hall of Fame," replied Lee. Isabelle and Lee are brother and sister. Lee was chosen to play first base in the series. "I hope you win a big trophy," said Isabelle.

Name _____ Date _____

Directions: The following story has been written as one long paragraph. Please read the story and put a capital **P** everywhere that a new paragraph should start.
HINT: Remember to make a new paragraph when the story switches to narration. There should be 12 paragraphs.

The Mysterious Bag
by Michael Anderson, age 10

"I'm going to a meeting and will be back in five minutes," said my teacher, Mr. Smith. As he left, he propped a paper bag up on his desk. About five minutes later, the bag moved. The whole class looked up. "Go touch it," said a girl sitting next to me. "OK," I said. I pushed my chair out from my desk and got up. I walked over to the desk and poked the bag. It started moving again. Then I opened it. There was a little animal, but it was only a couple of inches tall. It raised its arms, and I picked it up. Jacquez screamed, "AHHHH! Are you crazy, Michael?" I looked back inside the bag. There was a little chest small enough to fit in the palm of a hand. "I wonder what that is," I thought. Then I saw the animal I had taken out of the bag. It had grown, but not just a little bit! It was as big as my desk. The only thing I could find in my voice was "Oh, no!" I ran to the bag and opened the chest. There was honey in it. I fed it to the animal. Just then, Mr. Smith walked in. "What are you doing?" asked Mr. Smith. "Mr. Smith," I said, smiling my nicest smile. "Was this supposed to be for science class?"

This homework is due at school on _____ .

_____   _____
Child's signature   Parent's signature

 Week-by-Week Homework for Building Grammar, Usage, and Mechanics Skills © 2010 by Mary Rose, Scholastic Teaching Resources

Name _____ Date _____

Directions: Read the following story. Add commas and quotation marks where you think they should go. Put a capital **P** where you think a new paragraph should begin.

Please take these papers to the office said Mrs. Miller. I picked up the papers and started out of the door. And hurry back, because it is almost time for our math test. OK I said. I was just walking down the hallway to the office, when I noticed that my shoe was untied. I bent down to tie it and noticed a small door. It was right beside the drinking fountain, but I had never noticed it before. I stooped down and went through it. What are you doing in here? cried a loud voice. No children are allowed here in the teachers' lounge. I knew I was in trouble when I saw it was Mr. Merkle. I am so sorry, I said. I was looking for the office. How do I get out of here? First, you give me that book, young man. What book? I am just taking papers to the office for Mrs. Miller. I don't see any papers. I only see a copy of a short story by Sherlock Holmes. Where did you get that? I am missing a copy of this book from my classroom. I have no idea, Mr. Merkle. I only know that I went through a little door. Well, you had best get back through that door right now. I walked slowly toward the soda machine and was suddenly back in the hallway tying my shoe. I looked down and saw Mrs. Miller's papers. I hurried to the office and then back to class just in time to hear, Get out a paper and pencil for the math test. What a crazy day!

Capitalization

There are 34 main rules for using capital letters, but we will focus only on the dozen or so that are the most important for students to know.

Overview of the Skills

Lesson #1

Use capital letters for proper nouns, titles of respect, and the personal pronoun _I_.

This lesson should be easy for your students. They should have learned in the early grades to capitalize proper nouns, such as the names of people and pets; brand and store names; titles of respect, such as _Dr._ and _Mrs._; and names of cities, states, and countries.

To teach this lesson, simply point out examples found in literature or content area reading. You might also retype a selection with capitalization errors and ask students to fix them. They can work with partners or self-correct by checking against the original passage.

Lesson #2

Use capitals to begin sentences and for days of the week, months, and names of holidays.

This should also be an easy lesson and a great review for your students. Let them enjoy this quick and simple homework lesson— and an easy "A."

Lesson #3

Use capital letters for the names of places, buildings, and monuments; for street and road names; and for names of bodies of water when used as proper nouns.

It can be confusing for students to capitalize "Lake" in one situation, but not in another. In general, if the word is part of a phrase that is a proper name, then the word is also capitalized: _I live on Lake Michigan_ vs. *I live on a lake.* This lesson provides clear examples of when common nouns like *ocean*, *lake*, and *street* do and do not need capital letters. Here's a brief list of sample situations:

* *We visit a national park each summer. Our favorite is Yellowstone National Park.*
* *Jim lives on Elm Street. It is a very quiet street.*
* *I like to swim in the ocean. I swim in the Atlantic Ocean.*

Lesson #4

Use capitals for words for types of relatives when they are used as a name: *grandmother* vs. *Grandmother*.

We have lots of relatives: mom, dad, grandmother, grandfather, uncle, aunt, cousin, niece, and nephew. If the "relative" word is used in place of a name, it gets a capital. (*I will give the paper to Mom*; *Mom* is used in place of her real name, which is "Nancy.") The "relative" word is also capitalized if it comes with the person's actual name. (*Aunt Nancy is my favorite relative. Grandpa Joe has a big farm.*) We capitalize the relative word when it is the name we call that person: *May I have another cookie, Grandmother?* Note that we do not capitalize in this situation: *My grandmother lives in Ohio.*

In fact, we usually do not capitalize the relative word if it is preceded by a pronoun (I want to visit *my grandfather*) because we are simply stating the type of relative, not actually writing the name we call that person. Help students with this rule by posting a list of examples for reference, including:

* *My uncle owns a bike shop. We visit Uncle Bill at his shop every week.*
* *Who is your favorite aunt? My favorite aunt is Aunt Margo.*

Lesson #5

Use capitals with direction words when they name a region.

"Region" refers to the North, South, East, and West. We do not capitalize these if we are using them as a direction. (*You need to drive south for six blocks. The shop is just west of the park.*) However, we do capitalize these terms when they are being used as the name for an area. (*My sister lives in the North.*) A good trick that works most of the time is to look for the definite article, *the*. If *the* precedes the direction word, then the direction word usually needs a capital letter. (*My cousin lives in the Northeast. Cactus plants grow in the Southwest.*)

HINT: This "definite-article" test does not tend to work if the sentence includes the word *part*, or if the direction word ends with *-ern*, as in *western* and *northeastern*. (*The northwestern part of the United States is beautiful.*)

Name _____ Date _____

Directions: Write the word in parentheses into the space in the sentence. Use capital letters when necessary.

1. My family used to live in the _____. (northeast)

2. New Hampshire is _____ of Kentucky. (northeast)

3. I live on Elm _____. (street)

4. My family likes to visit the _____ each summer. (ocean)

5. Last year, we sailed on the _____. (atlantic ocean)

6. I love to eat a _____ with ketchup and pickles. (burger)

7. When _____ Jake came to see me, he brought me a kite. (uncle)

8. My _____ and I went to get some ice cream. (uncle)

9. My dentist is named _____ Lang. (doctor)

10. I had to go to the _____ last week. (doctor)

11. My birthday is on _____. (valentine's day)

12. I used to have a dog named _____. (sandy)

13. The state of _____ has a beautiful coastline. (oregon)

14. Thanksgiving is in _____. (november)

15. Halloween comes in _____ (october), a fall _____. (month)

Week-by-Week Homework for Building Grammar, Usage, and Mechanics Skills © 2010 by Mary Rose, Scholastic Teaching Resources

Dear Families,

Every letter in our alphabet can be made as an uppercase (capital) or lowercase letter. The sentence you are reading right now has only one capital, the letter *T*. There are 34 rules of capitalization. Happily, this homework lesson focuses on easy rules that your child probably already knows.

Capitalization of proper nouns, titles of respect, and the personal pronoun *I*

* **Use a capital (uppercase) letter for proper nouns:**

  - names of people and pets *(Theresa* and *Snuggles)*
  - store and brand names *(Home Depot, Kellogg's cereal, Kleenex tissue)*
  - titles of respect *(Ms. Kinney, Mr. Morris, Dr. Blake)*
  - names of cities, states, and countries *(Detroit, Michigan; London, England)*

* **Use a capital for the personal pronoun *I*.**

We did this in class!

Directions: Write the word in parentheses on the line provided. Use capital letters when necessary. HINT: Sometimes you should just rewrite the word and NOT use a capital.

1. My dentist is named _____ .
   (doctor smith)

2. He lives in _____ , _____ .
   (omaha, nebraska)

3. On Tuesday, _____ visited my aunt in _____ , _____ .
   (i)   (dallas, texas)

4. _____ came home from _____
   (george)   (chicago)

   and brought me a _____ named _____ .
                      (cat)   (pebbles)

5. My _____ _____ likes to play piano.
       (sister)   (susan)

Name _____ Date _____

Directions: Write the words in parentheses on the lines provided. Use capital letters when necessary. Refer to the rules if you are unsure. HINT: Some of the words do NOT need a capital.

What is the number-one _____ chain in the world? If you
(fast-food)

guessed _____, then _____ guessed right. A man named
(mcdonald's)   (you)

_____ opened the first _____
(mr. ray kroc)   (mcdonald's)

restaurant in 1955. It was in _____, _____, near
(des plaines)   (illinois)

_____. He wanted to train his _____ to be clean,
(chicago)   (workers)

friendly, and _____, so he opened a school called _____
(organized)   (hamburger)

_____. At first, he sold his _____ for 15 cents.
(university)   (hamburgers)

Now, people all over the world enjoy _____ food. Today there are
(mcdonald's)

_____ in 100 countries, including _____ and _____.
(restaurants)   (india)   (china)

In _____, we love to visit _____
(america)   (fast-food)

restaurants—and the one with the golden _____ is our favorite.
(arches)

· ·

This homework is due at school on _____ .

_____   _____
Child's signature   Parent's signature

Dear Families,

There are many instances where we need to use capital letters. This lesson covers words and rules children see and use frequently.

* **Use a capital letter to begin every sentence.**

* **Use a capital letter for days of the week, the names of months, and holidays.** *(Monday, February, Valentine's Day)*

Capital letters to begin sentences, for days of the week, and for names of months and holidays

We did this in class!

Directions: Use a calendar and your imagination to answer the following questions. Please use complete sentences and refer to the rules above to see where to make capital letters.

1. In what month were you born?

_____

2. What is your favorite holiday?

_____

3. What day of the week is it today?

_____

4. What are the names of the summer months?

_____

5. What holidays are in the fall?

_____

Name _____ Date _____

Directions: Read the following sentences about a holiday. Then rewrite the paragraph and include capital letters where they should have been used.

national peanut day is celebrated on september 13. actually, peanuts are not nuts. they are called "legumes" and are like peas and beans. peanuts are quite good for you. they are high in protein and fiber, and because they fill you up quickly, you tend to eat less. you may want to celebrate this day and also national peanut butter lovers' day on march 1. in 2011, national peanut butter lovers' day will be on a tuesday. it will be the perfect day for you to get out a jar of jif or peter pan peanut butter and make yourself a sandwich. don't forget the grape jelly!

_____

_____

_____

_____

_____

_____

_____

_____

_____

_____

This homework is due at school on _____.

_____   _____
Child's signature   Parent's signature

Dear Families,

The rules of capitalization can be very simple, yet very confusing for children. The easier ones are clear: Use an uppercase letter for proper nouns and to begin every sentence. Here, we will focus on one of the more difficult rules of capitalization:

* **Use capitals for names of places, buildings, and monuments; street and road names; and names of bodies of water when used as proper nouns.**

Look at these two sentences:

*My house is beside a **lake**. My house is beside **Lake Windsor**.*

In the first sentence, the word *lake* does not need a capital letter because it is not part of a name. In the second sentence, *lake* is part of the total name, *Lake Windsor*. You need to use uppercase letters if the word is part of a title or name of something.

HINT: See what the following sentences have in common with the example above and find a pattern that will help you always get these correct.

*My friend lives near **Port Angeles**. The cruise ship was docked at a **port**.*

Capitalization of the names of places, buildings, and monuments; street and road names; and names of bodies of water when used as proper nouns

We did this in class!

Directions: Write the word in parentheses on the line provided. Use capital letters when necessary. HINT: Sometimes you will write the word and NOT use a capital letter.

1. People often walk across the Brooklyn _____. (bridge)

2. The _____ goes from Manhattan to Brooklyn. (bridge)

3. The _____ is full of fish. (pond)

4. Walden _____ is very famous. (pond)

5. Our family went to Salt _____ City, Utah. (lake)

6. The water in the _____ is very salty. (lake)

7. They are paving the _____ in front of our school. (road)

8. The jewelry store is located on Ivanhoe _____. (road)

Name _____ Date _____

**Families,
please help!**

Directions: Write the word in parentheses on the line provided.
Use capital letters when necessary. HINT: Sometimes you will just
rewrite the word and NOT use a capital letter.

1. What is the tallest _____ in Cleveland? (building)

2. The Empire State _____ is in New York City. (building)

3. We went to Central _____. (park)

4. We went to the _____ for a concert. (park)

5. Mom used the drive-through window at our _____. (bank)

6. We keep our money in The Farmer's _____. (bank)

7. The Platte _____ is in Nebraska. (river)

8. There is a _____ of rain pouring off our roof. (river)

9. The little girl pretended to be a _____. (queen)

10. The Delta _____ is a famous paddle-wheel boat. (queen)

11. Many small towns have a _____ called Main _____. (street, street)

12. The _____ was full of screaming football fans. (field)

13. The Chicago Cubs play at Wrigley _____. (field)

14. Virginia touches the Atlantic _____. (ocean)

15. We have to cross an _____ to get to France. (ocean)

. . . .

This homework is due at school on _____ .

_____   _____
Child's signature   Parent's signature

Week-by-Week Homework for Building Grammar, Usage, and Mechanics Skills © 2010 by Mary Rose, Scholastic Teaching Resources

Dear Families,

Certain rules of capitalization are confusing for children and adults alike. For example, when do we capitalize *grandmother, aunt,* or *uncle*? This homework will help your child learn these tricky rules of capitalization.

✱ **Use a capital letter for the "relative" word (*aunt, uncle, cousin*) when it is used as a name.**

HINT: Here are some ways you can tell when to capitalize: If you can substitute a person's real name and not change the rest of the sentence, the word probably needs a capital. Pretend your mother's name is Patsy. *I will help Patsy fold the laundry. I will help Mom fold the laundry. Mom* is used in place of *Patsy*, so use a capital letter.

If the relative word is preceded by a pronoun, such as *his, her,* or *my*, it usually needs a lowercase letter. *Tommy helped his uncle wash the car.* We cannot substitute a name and say, *Tommy helped his George wash the car.* However, if we refer to the uncle by name, we use a capital letter: *Tommy helped his Uncle George wash the car.* When we use *great* with the relative's name, such as *Great Aunt*, the *great* follows the same rule as *aunt: I have a great aunt named Matilda. My Great Aunt Matilda lives in Chicago.*

Capitalization of words for types of relatives when used as a name: *grandmother* vs. *Grandmother*

We did this in class!

Directions: Read each sentence. Pay attention to the words that refer to relatives. Decide whether the sentence uses correct capitalization, then write *correct* or *incorrect* on the line. If incorrect, show how to fix it.

1. My aunt is named Carol. _____

2. Aunt Carol is my mother's sister. _____

3. His Uncle Jake is stationed in New Jersey. _____

4. Last summer, Donna went to visit Grandmother in North Carolina. _____

5. Donna enjoyed the visit with her Grandmother. _____

Name _____ Date _____

Directions: Read each sentence. Pay attention to the words that refer to relatives. Decide whether the sentence uses correct capitalization, then write *correct* or *incorrect* on the line. If incorrect, show how to fix it.

1. My grandmother is a good cook.   _____

2. Did you know grandmother gave me a new necklace?   _____

3. Luke went to visit his Uncle Herbert and Aunt Matilda.   _____

4. Uncle Herbert and Aunt Matilda gave Luke some presents.   _____

5. One day, grandfather taught Marco how to bait a fishing hook.   _____

6. Marco showed his grandfather how to reel in a big one.   _____

7. We were late for school because Mom could not find her car keys. _____

8. Dad brought the keys to our mom so we could get to school.   _____

9. My teacher said Mother is coming to parent conference night.   _____

10. Mrs. Hogan wants to have a conference with my Father.   _____

11. I am the Nephew of my Uncle Fred.   _____

12. Their aunt and uncle are coming for Thanksgiving.   _____

• •

This homework is due at school on _____ .

_____   _____
Child's signature   Parent's signature

Dear Families,

Among the rules for capitalization is one about the names of directions and regions. Many adults get this incorrect, so you know this one can be tough.

* **Use capitals for the names of directions when they name a region.**

If the direction word is used as a name, then it needs a capital letter. If it is just telling a direction, then it does not. Here are some examples:

* *New York City is located in the <u>Northeast</u>.*

   You will drive <u>north</u> two blocks to get to the stadium.

* *Hurricane Katrina hit the <u>South</u> very hard.*

   Many <u>southern</u> states had great amounts of damage.

   Cincinnati is in the <u>southwestern</u> part of Ohio.

* *The <u>West</u> contains states like California, Oregon, and Washington.*

* *Many prestigious colleges are located in the <u>East</u>.*

HINT: Look at the sentences that have an asterisk (*). In these sentences, the direction words are capitalized. Can you find what they have in common? What word comes right before the direction word? Keep in mind that we do not use capitals if the direction includes the word *part* or ends with *-ern*, as in *western* and *northeastern*.

Capitalization of direction words when they name a region

....

We did this in class!

Directions: Write the words in parentheses on the lines provided. Use capital letters when necessary.

1. Disney World is in the _____ part of Orlando. (southern)

2. Indiana is in the heart of the _____. (midwest)

3. You would drive _____ from San Diego to San Francisco. (north)

4. Those tomatoes were grown in the _____. (north)

5. My family wanted to travel in the _____ states. (northeastern)

6. The Mississippi river runs _____ to _____. (north, south)

Name _____ Date _____

Families, please help!

Directions: Write the words in parentheses on the lines provided. Use capital letters when necessary.

1. Lewis and Clark traveled to the _____. (northwest)

2. Columbus sailed from _____ to _____. (east, west)

3. The _____ point in the United States is Key West. (southernmost)

4. The Wilsons moved from the _____ to the _____. (east, west)

5. The great American deserts are located in the _____. (southwest)

6. Oranges are grown in the _____. (south)

7. Times Square is _____ of Harlem. (south)

8. Tim grew up in the _____. (midwest)

9. Those are _____ tomatoes. (midwestern)

10. A compass needle always points to the _____. (north)

11. Look _____ to see the rainbow. (east)

12. Orchids like to grow in a _____ window. (northern)

13. Georgia is located in the _____. (southeast)

14. Canada is _____ of the United States. (north)

15. My computer was shipped here from down _____. (south)

• •

This homework is due at school on _____ .

_____   _____
Child's signature   Parent's signature

Review: Capitalization

Name _____ Date _____

Directions: Write the words in parentheses on the lines provided. Use capital letters when necessary. HINT: Sometimes you should just rewrite the word and NOT use a capital.

What Do You Know About Our States?

Pennsylvania is located in the _____. The _____ has 45,000
(northeast)   (state)

square miles of land, and the capital is _____. It is famous for
(harrisburg)

_____ and _____.
(livestock)   (steel)

_____ is located in the _____ of our country. It has the
(oklahoma)   (center)

_____ _____ _____ ____ _____.
(national) (cowboy)   (hall) (of) (fame)

The _____ _____ is held in _____ each year.
(state)   (fair)   (september)

Texas is located _____ of _____. _____
(south)   (oklahoma)   (texas)

is the home of the _____. On _____, _____ 23, 1836,
(alamo)   (tuesday) (february)

there was a battle that made this building famous.

Vermont is the _____ _____ _____.
(green)   (mountain)   (state)

My _____ lives there. I go for a visit every _____, but this year, _____
(sister)   (summer)   (i)

am going to see her at _____.
(christmastime)

_____ is one of our largest _____. It is in the
(california)   (states)

_____ part of the _____ _____.
(western)   (united)   (states)

Spelling

Spelling comes easy for some, but for most of us, there are at least a few words that cause confusion. There are rules we can follow, but the exceptions to the rules are many. This section will outline some rules, clarify some commonly confused words, and help students come up with their own spelling tricks for "tricky" words.

Tip

When doing the Spelling Assessment, read the sentences out loud, speaking (but not spelling) the words students need to spell. You'll find the word list in the Answer Key (page 96).

Overview of the Skills

Lesson # 1

Common mix-ups: *there/their/they're*

Begin with a quick lesson in which you point out that *the, they, there, their,* and *they're* all begin with the same three letters! Just teaching this may help with the *they/thay* errors that crop up in student writing. Then move on to our main focus: *their, they're,* and *there*. Dissect the three words and teach these tricks.

There (in that place) contains the word *here*, so use *there* when writing about a place.

Their (belonging to them) contains the word *heir*. A quick glance in the dictionary will help students discover that *heir* has to do with ownership. We use *their* to show ownership.

Finally, remind students that *they're* is a contraction. Have them read *they're* as the two words from which the contraction was formed. If *they are* fits in the sentence, then *they're* is the correct word to use. (*They're coming to the game tonight. They are coming to the game tonight.*)

Lesson # 2

Common mix-ups: *your/you're*

To teach the difference between *your* and *you're*, you can use methods similar to those for *their* and *they're*.

Point out that when we look at the word *your*, we can see the word *our* hiding inside of it. *Our* refers to ownership, so we use *your* to show ownership. (*Bring your math book to class.*)

Remind students that *you're* has an apostrophe and is a contraction for *you are*. When writing, students should remember to read *you're* as the two words it represents. If *you are* works, then *you're* is the right word to use. (*You're going to be late for class. You are going to be late for class.*)

Lesson #3

Silent consonants: letters we do not pronounce, like the *s* in *island*

A, e, i, o, u, and sometimes *y* are vowels. The other letters are consonants. Many words contain silent consonants—like the *s* in *island* or the *t* in *filet*—that make spelling difficult.

Point out to students that in American English, we do not to pronounce the *l* in *salmon* or the *t* in *often*! Add other silent-consonant words to the list: *sign, aisle, campaign, write, wrote, wrong, wrist, pledge, knee, know, rhyme.* Better yet, have students be on the lookout for more words with silent letters and list these on the board. Create a "Silent Letter Chart" and encourage students to add words with silent letters to the chart. It has far more impact when they do it themselves!

Lesson #4

Homophones: words that sound alike but are spelled differently

There are pages and pages of words that could have made their way into this lesson. Included here are those that are used most often and confused most often by elementary students. Write the words below on the board and discuss the different meanings of the words. Encourage students to come up with additional homophones.

bow, bough	*threw, through*	*to, too, two*
claws, clause	*weak, week*	*tale, tail*
brake, break	*hear, here*	*our, hour*

Have students make a list of homophones and their meanings and keep it in their writing folders. Make a bulletin board, too, and challenge students to add to it.

Lesson #5

Memory tricks for correct spelling of confusing words

This lesson deals with commonly misspelled words and some memory tricks to help students (and adults!) remember the correct spelling. For example:

* *February* (not *Febuary*)—*Brr! It's cold in February.* Say "Febrrruary," and you'll get it right.

* *Wednesday* (not *Wensday*)—*She will wed next Wednesday.* Remembering this sentence will help you remember the silent *d.*

As you encounter new hard-to-spell words in your class, encourage students to come up with their own memory tricks, or mnemonic devices, to help them remember the correct spelling.

Name _____ Date _____

Directions: This is actually a spelling quiz, so please listen carefully to the sentences as your teacher reads them aloud. Pay special attention to spelling when you fill in the blanks.
HINT: Teachers, the word list is in the Answer Key (page 96).

1. The Legos were stuck together so it was hard to _____ them.

2. The children were afraid of the closet, so they never went in _____.

3. Marcus set each place at the table with a napkin, a fork, a _____, and a spoon.

4. Jamaica raised her hand because she knew the _____ to the question.

5. The town built a new _____ across the river.

6. We went to _____ the ship sail out to _____.

7. I _____ you when you say that winter is your favorite time of year.

8. Don't forget to bring _____ homework to school in the morning.

9. The _____ on the highway said to exit here for Route 66.

10. Today is Sunday. _____ is Monday.

11. _____ teacher read for a long time today. Her story lasted almost an _____.

12. The leader of our school is Mr. Rowland, the _____.

13. Joey is naughty a lot, and he _____ gets in trouble.

14. Watch where _____ going, Jennifer, or you will fall!

15. What a great surprise! All of the students remembered _____ homework today!

Week-by-Week Homework for Building Grammar, Usage, and Mechanics Skills © 2010 by Mary Rose, Scholastic Teaching Strategies

Dear Families,

Almost every student gets confused about when to use the familiar words *there*, *their*, and *they're*. This lesson offers some hints to help your child remember when to use each one. Please go over these simple strategies with your child, then help him or her complete the sentences on the next page.

❋ **Use *there* to refer to a place. Use *their* to show ownership. *They're* is a contraction for *they are*.**

Look carefully at the word *there*. Notice that it contains the word *here*. Both *here* and *there* are places. This should help your child remember that *there* refers to a place. "Don't go in there!" means "Do not go in that place!"

Do you know the meaning of the word *heir*? It refers to a person who will get to own something that a parent or relative now has. The word *their* contains the word *heir*. We use *their* when talking about ownership. "That is their new car."

When you see *they're*, you see the apostrophe that signals it is a contraction—two words shortened into one. Write *they're* when you mean *they are*. "They're sitting on the bus."

**Common mix-ups:
*there / their / they're***

We did this in class!

Directions: Write either *there*, *their*, or *they're* in each space below.

1. Put the papers in the box over _____.

   (Remember that "in the box" is a PLACE.)

2. The children looked at _____ shoes to see who had tracked in the mud.

   (Do they OWN the shoes?)

3. The two birds were building _____ nest to get ready for baby birds.

   (A little tricky, but remember that if they build it, they probably own it!)

4. It is really cold out _____. *(Outside is a place!)*

5. _____ working hard on their homework.

   (What do you really mean to say? Is it two words?)

Name _____ Date _____

Directions: Write either *there*, *their*, or *they're* in each space below. Refer to the front of this sheet for hints about which word to use.

1. We will listen at the door to see what _____ talking about.

2. They may be talking about _____ Halloween costumes.

3. Let's put the costumes over _____.

4. Is _____ a good place to keep our masks for trick-or-treating?

5. The children got _____ bags ready to collect Halloween candy.

6. _____ beginning to get excited about the big night.

7. Finally, it is time to go out _____ and ring doorbells!

8. The Smiths were home. We rang the doorbell of _____ house.

9. The friendly people will open _____ door and give us candy.

10. _____ surprised by our amazing costumes.

· ·

This homework is due at school on _____.

_____   _____
            Child's signature   Parent's signature

Dear Families,

Practically every child has trouble deciding when to use *your* and when to use *you're*. This lesson will help your child make that choice easily and correctly.

✳ **Use *your* to show ownership. *You're* is a contraction
for "you are."**

The word *your* denotes ownership. One trick to help you remember this is that *your* contains the word *our*, which means that we own something. "That is your book."

You're is a contraction—two words that have been contracted, or shortened, into one word. We use *you're* when we are saying *you are*. If you are not sure which one to use, read the sentence out loud with the words *you are* and see if it makes sense. "You're in school. You are in school."

**Common mix-ups:
*your/you're***

....

**We did this
in class!**

Directions: Write *you're* or *your* in each of the following sentences. HINT: It will help to read them aloud and say "you are" when you come to the space. If *you are* makes sense, choose the contraction, *you're*. If it doesn't make sense, choose *your*, then check to see if the sentence expresses ownership.

1. Think about _____ vacation. (Does *you are vacation* make sense?)

2. _____ going to write a story about it today. (Does *you are going to* make sense?)

3. _____ story should be three pages long.

4. _____ also going to draw pictures to go with _____ story.

5. Then you will read _____ story out loud to _____ friends.

6. I hope _____ proud of _____ work.

Name _____ Date _____

Directions: Write *you're* or *your* in each of the following sentences. HINT: It will help to read them aloud and say "you are" when you come to the space. If *you are* makes sense, choose the contraction, *you're*. If it doesn't make sense, choose *your*, then check to see if the sentence expresses ownership.

Ready for School?

1. Don't forget to make _____ bed before you leave this house.

2. If you don't hurry, _____ going to be late for school.

3. Please eat _____ breakfast slowly or _____ going to choke.

4. Remember to take _____ backpack to school.

5. _____ visiting _____ grandmother after school today.

6. Do you have _____ homework?

7. Please give _____ lunch money to _____ teacher.

8. If you don't tie _____ shoes, _____ going to trip and fall.

9. Do you think _____ class will go outside to play today?

10. Take _____ violin out to the car.

11. Don't forget that _____ taking your sister to kindergarten.

12. Fasten _____ seatbelt.

• •

This homework is due at school on _____ .

_____   _____
Child's signature   Parent's signature

Week-by-Week Homework for Building Grammar, Usage, and Mechanics Skills © 2010 by Mary Rose, Scholastic Teaching Resources

Dear Families,

Spelling Lesson #3

Although we sometimes pronounce words differently in different parts of our country, the words below all have something in common: "silent consonants." That means some letters are silent, and we do not pronounce them. There are 26 letters in the English alphabet. The vowels are *a, e, i, o, u,* and sometimes *y.* All the other letters are consonants.

* **Silent consonants are consonant letters that we do not pronounce in a word. *Island* contains a silent *s.***

Today's homework will deal with familiar words that contain a silent letter. Examples include the word *knee* (pronounced *nee*) and *doubt* (*dowt*).

Silent consonants: letters we do not pronounce, like the *s* in *island*

We did this in class!

Directions: Here is a list of some words with silent consonants. Use words from the list to fill in the blanks below. Check for correct spelling. Circle the letter or letters that are not pronounced.

answer	caught	doubt	honest	knife	sign
autumn	comb	foreign	hour	ledge	solemn
bought	debt	ghost	island	receipt	thought
bridge	depot	high	knee	salmon	through

1. We will have _____ for supper tonight.

2. You can cross that _____ when you come to it.

3. We looked _____ and low for the car keys.

4. At Halloween, Tommy was a scary, white _____.

5. Susan fell down and skinned her _____.

6. We _____ our new stove at Home _____.

Week-by-Week Homework for Building Grammar, Usage, and Mechanics Skills © 2010 by Mary Rose, Scholastic Teaching Resources

73

Name _____ Date _____

Directions: Here is a list of some words with silent consonants. Use words from the list to fill in the blanks below. Check for correct spelling. Circle the letter or letters that are not pronounced.

answer	caught	doubt	honest	knife	sign
autumn	comb	foreign	hour	ledge	solemn
bought	debt	ghost	island	receipt	thought
bridge	depot	high	knee	salmon	through

1. Our cruise ship stopped so we could visit an _____.

2. Last summer, I _____ eleven fish.

3. Please _____ your hair.

4. Greece is a _____ country.

5. The _____ on the door says "EXIT."

6. Please _____ every question on the test.

7. Our school will start in the _____.

8. If you owe someone money, we say you have a _____ to pay.

9. Joe's mother _____ new school clothes for him.

10. Please be _____ and never lie to your friends.

This homework is due at school on _____ .

_____   _____
Child's signature   Parent's signature

Dear Families,

Perhaps there is no part of our language more puzzling to a beginning reader and writer than homophones.

* **Homophones are two words that sound alike, but are spelled differently. (claws/clause; heal/heel; see/sea)**

Please be patient as your child works on this homework assignment. Remember that in this lesson, unlike others, reading out loud will not help! Your child must read, look carefully at the word, and make the right choice.

Homophones: words that sound alike but are spelled differently

---

We did this in class!

Directions: Look at the homophone pairs. Choose the correct word and write it in the blank.

1. **(blew/blue)**   My favorite color is _____.

   The wind _____ all evening long.

2. **(ate/eight)**   I have _____ brothers and sisters.

   I _____ ice cream after dinner.

3. **(peace/piece)**   I want a _____ of your candy.

   I enjoyed the _____ and quiet of the garden.

4. **(flour/flower)**   My mother uses _____ to make cookies.

   I brought my mother a pretty _____ for her birthday.

5. **(sail/sale)**   I got these shoes at a _____ price.

   The captain ordered that the _____ should go up.

6. **(cent/scent/sent)**   I found a _____ (penny) on the sidewalk.

   I _____ my little brother outside.

   I noticed the _____ of pancakes when I woke up.

Name _____ Date _____

Families, please help!

Directions: Look at the homophone pairs. Choose the correct word and write it in the blank. Please use a dictionary if you are unsure.

1. **(heal/heel)**   I cut the _____ of my foot on a piece of glass.

   The doctor said it will _____ quickly.

2. **(threw/through)** Oops! I _____ the ball _____ the window.

3. **(week/weak)**   Someone who is not strong is _____.

   Friday is my favorite day of the _____.

4. **(tail/tale)**   Have you read *The* _____ *of Peter Rabbit*?

   The monkey had a long, curved _____.

5. **(break/brake)** Do you have a hand _____ on your bike?

   Be careful not to _____ your glasses.

6. **(hear/here)**   Can you _____ the music on your iPod?

   Please keep your iPod in _____.

7. **(seen/scene)**   Have you _____ the new Harry Potter movie?

   My favorite _____ is when he meets Voldemort.

8. **(to/too/two)**   If you are going _____ the movies, I want to go, _____.

   These cookies are small, so you can have _____.

· ·

This homework is due at school on _____.

_____   _____
        Child's signature   Parent's signature

Spelling Lesson #4

Dear Families,

Most of us have a few words that we just can't seem to remember how to spell. As adults, we resort to writing the words to see if they look correct, looking them up in a dictionary, asking a friend for help, or perhaps choosing a different word altogether! There are certain words that are commonly misspelled, so this lesson will focus on using tricks to remember the correct spelling of these words. Check these out, and try coming up with your own memory tricks to help your child with his or her weekly spelling lists!

Memory tricks for correct spelling of confusing words

✱ **Use memory tricks to spell common tricky words correctly.**

- *February* (not *Febuary*)–*Brr! It's cold in February.* Say "Fe*brrr*uary," and you will get it right.

- *Wednesday* (not *Wensday*)–*She will wed next Wednesday.* Remember this sentence and you'll remember the silent *d.*

We did this in class!

Directions: Work with other students to develop tricks to remember how to spell these words. Write the trick on the lines provided.

calendar (Most kids spell it with *-er* at the end; this is incorrect.)

_____

congratulations (Most kids spell it with a *d* in place of the first letter *t.*)

_____

supposed (*Supposed* often goes with *to,* as in "He is supposed to be at school." Many students forget the *d* at the end of the word.)

_____

Name _____ Date _____

Directions: Here is a list of commonly misspelled words and the memory tricks to help you get the correct spelling. Choose from this list to fill in the blanks—and watch your spelling!

Believe	Don't be**lie**ve a **lie**. (Use *i* before *e*.)
Vacuum	Vac**uu**m **u**p **u**nder the sofa. (Use *u* two times in a row.)
Thief	A th**ie**f will **lie**. (*i* before *e*, as in *lie*.)
Separate	Drat! There's **a rat** in sep**arat**e.
Burglar	The bur**glar** doesn't like the **glar**e of light.
Chocolate	I was **late**, so I ate all the choco**late**.
Weird	**We** are all **we**ird. (Start the word with *we*.)
Principal	The princi**pal** of your school is your **pal**.
Witch	The w**itch** scratched her **itch**.
Tomorrow	**Tom**, there will be no s**orrow tomorrow**.

1. The police finally caught the _____ who had stolen the car.

2. Please _____ the reading and math papers into two piles.

3. My favorite desserts contain _____.

4. I didn't like the movie. The story was strange and the characters were _____.

5. The _____ passed out awards at our school.

6. I had to clean my room and _____ the rug.

7. _____ is Saturday, so there will be no school.

· ·

This homework is due at school on _____ .

_____   _____
Child's signature   Parent's signature

Spelling Lesson #5

Week-by-Week Homework for Building Grammar, Usage, and Mechanics Skills © 2010 by Mary Rose, Scholastic Teaching Resources

Review: Spelling

I. Directions: Each of the following words is spelled incorrectly. Write the correct spelling in the space beside each word.

Febuary _____   wierd _____

tommorow _____   vacum _____

seperate _____   onest _____

beleive _____   brige _____

Wendesday _____   dout _____

calender _____   nife _____

II. Directions: Write *there*, *their*, *they're*, *your*, or *you're*, in each space below.

1. The children put _____ lab coats on for science class.

2. Mrs. Culp said, "Put the clip boards over _____."

3. She called Jamie and Julie to the front of the room. "_____ going to do a presentation of a volcano erupting," she said.

4. Everyone said, "Jamie and Julie, _____ project was great!"

5. Tomorrow, _____ going to do it for the whole school.

III. Directions: Circle the correct word or words in each sentence.

1. Logan (ate/eight) (ate/eight) Hershey Kisses this afternoon.

2. The sky was (blue/blew), and the wind (blue/blew).

3. Michael wanted a (piece/peace) of Logan's candy.

4. Logan (through/threw) some candy (through/threw) the air.

5. Bears have very sharp (claws/clause).

Word Choice

Professional writers know how important it is to use just-right words in just the right ways. To do that in their own writing, students need to know how to make good choices—and how to make correct choices, especially when it comes to tricky situations. This means using verb tenses correctly and checking for subject-verb agreement; making the best use of adjectives and forming them properly; and knowing when a word that may seem right is, frankly, wrong. That is what this Word Choice section is all about.

Overview of the Skills

Lesson # 1

Verb tenses: regular verbs

Every verb has three main tenses: present, past, and future. The present tense is used for actions taking place now or regularly. The past tense is used for things in the past, things that have already happened. The future is for things that will happen at a later date.

"Regular" verbs follow very regular rules to form tenses: They use the basic verb or add *-ing* for present tense; add either *-d* or *-ed* for past tense; and use a helping word, usually *will* or *shall,* for the future tense. *Look* and *play* are regular verbs and form tenses according to the rules:

Present	Past	Future
look/looking	*looked*	*will look*
play/playing	*played*	*will play*

Lesson #2

Verb tenses: irregular verbs

Irregular verbs form their past tenses in unpredictable ways. There are 90 common but tricky verbs, so be sure to continue teaching other irregular verbs throughout the year. Here are some examples of high-frequency irregular verbs:

Present	Past	Future
go/going	*went*	*will go*
run/running	*ran*	*will run*
eat/eating	*ate*	*will eat*

Since irregular verbs do not follow rules, kids just have to learn them. So make a class chart and add to it throughout the year!

Lesson #3
Subject-verb agreement

The rules are simple: A singular subject needs a singular verb; a plural subject needs a plural verb. Help students "discover" that, unlike for nouns, an *s* does NOT necessarily mean a verb is plural. In fact, adding an *s* to a verb usually means the subject is singular: *He **looks** at his watch all the time.* Remind students that we only use this *s* form for third-person singular subjects (things that are *he*, *she*, or *it*). Add to these examples and ask students to say which are singular and which are plural.

He runs fast. They run fast.
She enjoys math. They enjoy math.

The dog is chewing on bones.
They get the answers right every time.

Lesson #4
Choosing the correct word

The words in this lesson may seem to mean the same thing and be interchangeable, but they are not. Words like *can/may*, *less/fewer*, and *good/well*, for example, are similar in meaning but have specific situations in which each one is correct. There are well over 100 words that could go in this lesson, so continue to work on clarifying the use of other tricky words. Here are some to work on throughout the year: *affect/effect*; *allusion/illusion*; *command/commend*; *breath/breathe*; *farther/further*; *desert/dessert*; *lose/loose*; *quite/quiet*.

Lesson #5
Comparison of adjectives

Adjectives are words that modify nouns. They tell us whether something is big or little, wet or dry, young or old. When it comes to describing and comparing things with adjectives, there are three degrees of comparison: positive (*big*), comparative (*bigger*), and superlative (*biggest*). We use the positive form when talking about just one person or thing (She is *smart*); we use the comparative form to compare two things (She is *smarter* than her sister), and the superlative form to compare more than two things (She is the *smartest* girl in the family). Longer adjectives require the use of *more* to compare two things (He is *more* handsome than his brother), and *most* to compare more than two things (He is the *most* handsome man in the family).

Name _____ Date _____

I. Regular & Irregular Verb Tenses

Directions: Write the correct form of each verb in the space provided.

1. Mr. Harless (call) _____ Millie into his office yesterday.

2. He (say) _____ that she was going to get an award.

3. My mom and dad (come) _____ to watch me receive the award.

4. We (run) _____ to the car this morning because it was raining.

II. Subject-Verb Agreement   **Directions:** Circle the correct word for each sentence.

1. All of the scientists (hope/hopes) that the mission is a success.

2. The scientists (is/are) looking for dinosaurs.

3. Every scientist (need/needs) a logbook to record what she finds.

4. Each scientist (hope/hopes) to find something important.

III. Choose the Right Word   **Directions:** Circle the correct word for each sentence:

1. (Can/May) I listen to your iPod?

2. I am doing (well/good), now that I am over the flu.

3. Just pass it over to (me/myself).

4. I have (less/fewer) songs on my iPod than you do on yours.

IV. Comparison of Adjectives

Directions: Write the correct form of the word in the space provided.

1. Antarctica is the (cold) _____ place on Earth.

2. It is even (cold) _____ than the Arctic Circle.

3. Antarctica is also (dangerous) _____.

4. It is so cold, it is (dangerous) _____ than Alaska.

Dear Families,

Thank goodness for "regular" verbs! Regular verbs follow regular rules to form tenses: *past* (action that happened already), *present* (action happening now), and *future* (action that will take place later).

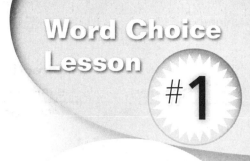
* **Regular verbs indicate present tense by adding *-ing* (or not changing the verb); by adding *-d* or *-ed* for past tense; and by using the helping words *shall* or *will* for the future tense.**

(FAMILIES, PLEASE NOTE: We will not deal with present-perfect, past-perfect, or future-perfect tenses in this lesson.)

....

We did this in class!

Directions: Look at the verb and subject below; then create three sentences using those words. One sentence should be in the present tense, one in the past tense, and one in the future tense.

EXAMPLE: **Verb: *bark*   Subject: *dog***

Past: _____The dog barked yesterday._____

Present: _The dog is barking now._____

Note also this present-tense form: *The dog barks.*

Future: __The dog will bark tomorrow._____

Verb: *listen*   Subject: *teacher*

(HINT: Because the teacher is the subject, it is the teacher who is listening.)

Past: _____

Present: _____

Future: _____

Name _____ Date _____

Families, please help!

Directions: Look at the verbs and subjects below, then create three sentences using those words. One sentence should be in the present tense, one in the past tense, and one in the future tense.

EXAMPLE: **Verb:** *jump*   **Subject:** *frog*

Past: _____ The frog jumped onto the lily pad. _____

Present: _____ The frog is jumping right now. _____

Future: _____ The frog will jump again tomorrow. _____

Verb: *smile*   **Subject:** *Samantha*

Past: _____

Present: _____

Future: _____

Verb: *kick*   **Subject:** *José*

Past: _____

Present: _____

Future: _____

. . . .

This homework is due at school on _____ .

_____   _____
Child's signature   Parent's signature

Word Choice Lesson #1

    Week-by-Week Homework for Building Grammar, Usage, and Mechanics Skills © 2010 by Mary Rose, Scholastic Teaching Resources

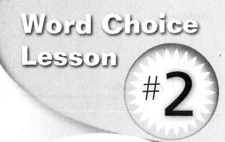

Dear Families,

The English language has strict rules for changing the tenses (past, present, and future times) of "regular" verbs, such as *look*. However, there are about 90 commonly used words that do not follow the rules. Fortunately, we learn these exceptions to the rules just by listening to language, by studying the verbs, and with the assistance of parents and teachers. This homework assignment deals with irregular verbs.

✳ **An irregular verb is one that forms tenses in unpredictable ways. We learn these irregular verbs by listening, reading, and practicing them.**

Verb tenses: irregular verbs

go
went
gone

We did this in class!

Directions: Draw a line to match the irregular verb to its past-tense form.

#	verb		past tense
1.	know		caught
2.	pay		read
3.	read		drove
4.	freeze		paid
5.	drive		knew
6.	catch		froze
7.	fall		swung
8.	write		fell
9.	think		wrote
10.	swing		thought

Name _____ Date _____

I. **Directions:** Draw a line to match the irregular verb to its past-tense form.

II. **Directions:** Write the past-tense forms of these common irregular verbs:

1.	hide		gave	**1.**	begin	_____
2.	leave		drew	**2.**	catch	_____
3.	bring		sang	**3.**	cut	_____
4.	lose		left	**4.**	teach	_____
5.	sing		brought	**5.**	think	_____
6.	stand		lost	**6.**	shake	_____
7.	swim		kept	**7.**	break	_____
8.	give		hid	**8.**	drink	_____
9.	draw		stood	**9.**	hold	_____
10.	keep		swam	**10.**	slide	_____

This homework is due at school on _____ .

_____ _____
Child's signature Parent's signature

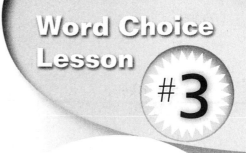

Dear Families,

Every sentence contains a subject and a verb. Certain verbs are "singular" (meaning one) and are used when we are talking about one subject. Certain verbs are plural (meaning more than one) and are used when the subject is more than one.

* **A singular subject requires a singular verb.**
  A plural subject requires a plural verb.
  When this is done correctly, we refer to this as "subject-verb agreement."

Look at this simple example: The child **is** reading a book. The children **are** reading books. *Child* is singular, meaning one child, so we use the singular verb *is*. The word *children* is plural, meaning several children, so we use the plural verb *are*.

HINT: Often a singular, present-tense verb will add an *s* to the end: *I run, he runs*; *you eat, she eats*; *I sleep, the cat sleeps*. Remember that this *s* does NOT mean a verb is plural.

Word Choice Lesson #3

Subject-verb agreement

We did this in class!

Directions: The subjects of these sentences are in bold print. On the space beside the number, put an **S** if the subject is singular, a **P** if it is plural. Then choose the correct verb.

1. ____ **They** (was/were) _____ the best players on the baseball team.

2. ____ **We** (is/are) _____ the winners of the league championship.

3. ____ **Bobby** (is/are) _____ the captain of the Reds baseball team.

4. ____ **I** (is/am) _____ the shortstop on the Cardinals team.

5. ____ The **players** (hit/hits) _____ the ball very hard.

6. ____ **Alex Rodriguez** (hit/hits) _____ a home run every week.

7. ____ **Susan and Linda** (read/reads) _____ every day.

8. ____ **Steven** (read/reads) _____ every day.

Name _____ Date _____

Families, please help!

I. Directions: The subjects of these sentences are in bold print. On the space beside the number, put an **S** if the subject is singular, a **P** if it is plural. Then write the correct verb form on the line.

1. ____ **Tommy** (whisper/whispers) _____ while he is reading.

2. ____ **Jake and Neil** (whisper/whispers) _____ during lunch.

3. ____ **Olivia and Gabriella** (watch/watches) _____ TV together.

4. ____ **Katrina** (watch/watches) _____ alone.

5. ____ **He** (think/thinks) _____ Spongebob is the best show.

6. ____ His **parents** (think/thinks) _____ Spongebob is the worst show.

II. Directions: Write your own sentences using the following subjects. Make sure your subject and your verb "agree."

1. Subject: *The children*   Verb: *need*

   _____

2. Subject: *Mrs. Johnson*   Verb: *like*

   _____

3. Subject: *The monkey*   Verb: *eat*

   _____

4. Subject: *The elephants*   Verb: *work*

   _____

· ·

This homework is due at school on _____ .

_____   _____
Child's signature   Parent's signature

Dear Families,

Certain words seem interchangeable but are <u>not</u>. As you read through these rules and examples, you'll probably find that you have heard these words used incorrectly before.

Choosing the correct word

* **can/may** *Can* means "to be able." *May* means "to have permission" or "be allowed."

  EXAMPLE: "I *can* write my name" means I *am able* to do this; I know how. "*May* I go to the movies?" means I am asking permission; I wonder if I am allowed to go.

* **wait on/wait for** *Wait on* means "to serve someone." *Wait for* means "expecting something to happen."

  EXAMPLE: If you say, "I am waiting on Joey to arrive," it means that you're standing on him! Most likely, you are not "waiting ON" Joey, but you are waiting FOR him to arrive. We "wait on" people when we work in a restaurant or store.

* **less/fewer** Use *fewer* if there is a definite number; if the quantity is countable. Use *less* for an amount that cannot be "counted."

  EXAMPLE: There are *fewer* kids in class today than yesterday. Carrots have *fewer* calories than cakes. (You can count the exact number of kids and calories.) I trust him *less* than his brother. (The amount of trust is *less*, but you can't give it a number.) The pool has *less* water now. (We can measure the amount of water, but we can't count water.)

* **good/well** *Good* is an adjective; *well* is an adverb.

  EXAMPLE: If someone asks, "How are you doing?" you should reply that you are "well" not "good." The question asks *how* you are *doing* (*doing* is a verb), so it calls for an adverb (*well*). An adverb modifies a verb. *Good* is an adjective. An adjective modifies a noun. You are a *good* person, but you feel *well*.

* **healthy/healthful** *Healthy* is "to have good health"; *healthful* is "to provide good health."

  EXAMPLE: People often say, "An apple is *healthy*." This is incorrect; apples do not have health. People and animals can be healthy. "An apple is a *healthful* food," is correct because an apple can provide good health.

* **me/myself** *Myself* cannot be used as the subject of a sentence or in place of the word *I* or *me*.

  EXAMPLE: *Wrong:* The teacher and myself were in the room. *Right:* The teacher and I were in the room. *Wrong:* Give the papers to Mr. Jones or myself. *Right:* Give the papers to Mr. Jones or me. **Note:** You can use *myself* this way: *I made it myself.*

We did this in class!   Our class went over all of the above rules. Please use these rules as a guide to do the homework.

Name _____ Date _____

Directions: Refer to the rules and examples on the back of this page to help you choose the correct word to put into each sentence.

1. **(can/may)** _____ I go over to Janie's house? I _____ make my own bed.

2. **(wait on/wait for)** I will _____ my mom to pick me up.

   I hope the waiter will _____ us soon.

3. **(less/fewer)** I have _____ homework than I did last week.

   I have _____ pieces of candy than you have.

4. **(good/well)** I can sing very _____. (HINT: *Singing* is a verb!)

   I think you are a _____ singer. (HINT: A *singer* is a person, a noun.)

5. **(healthy/healthful)** I have a very _____ cat named Cob.

   I ate a _____ breakfast this morning.

6. **(me/myself)** Please give the lunch money to _____.

   I would like to count it _____.

7. **(less/fewer)** This book has _____ pages than that one.

   The glass has _____ water than the bottle.

8. **(I/me/myself)** Either Jacob or _____ will bring the cake to the party.

   I will make the cake _____.

. . . .

This homework is due at school on _____ .

_____   _____
    Child's signature   Parent's signature

Dear Families,

When comparing things, we talk in "degrees." There are three degrees of comparison: *positive* (great), *comparative* (greater), and *superlative* (greatest). We add *-er* for comparatives and *-est* for superlatives. For adjectives ending in *-y*, we often change the *y* to *i*, and add *-er* or *-est* (*happy, happier, happiest*). Use *more* or *most* with longer adjectives (*beautiful, more beautiful, most beautiful*). Of course, some adjectives are irregular and don't follow any rules (*good, better, best*).

Comparison of adjectives

* **Use the *positive* degree when speaking of one thing.** (The movie was *long*.)

* **Use the *comparative* degree when comparing two things.** (The first movie was *longer* than the second.)

* **Use the *superlative* degree when comparing more than two things.** (That was the *longest* movie I have ever seen!)

We did this in class!

Directions: Look at the adjectives in boldface. Write the correct form of the adjective in the space provided. (HINT: For some, you may have to change a *y* to *i*; for others, you may need to use *more* or *most*.) Refer to the rules above and look out for exceptions to the rules!

1. wet   The grass is _____. It is _____ now than it was this morning.

2. warm   The blueberry pancakes were _____.

They were _____ than the oatmeal pancakes.

The buckwheat pancakes were the _____ of them all.

3. sunny   Today is _____. It is _____ today than yesterday.

The weatherman says that tomorrow will be the _____ day this week.

4. cooperative   Janet was _____ in science class today.

Ginny was _____ than Janet.

Martha was the _____ of all the girls.

5. colorful   Sebastian found a _____ butterfly.

Mark found one that was _____ than Sebastian's.

Greg found the _____ butterfly of all.

Name _____ Date _____

Directions: Write the correct form of the adjective in the space provided. (HINT: You might have to change a *y* to *i*; use *more* or *most*; or leave the word just as it is.) Refer to the rules on the back of this page and look out for exceptions to the rules!

1. **soft**   Papa Bear's bed was _____.

                      Mama Bear's bed was _____ than Papa Bear's.

                      Baby Bear's bed was the _____ of all three.

2. **comfortable**   Papa Bear's chair was _____.

                      Mama Bear's chair was _____ than Papa Bear's.

                      Baby Bear's chair was the _____.

3. **playful**   My cat is _____ than your cat.

4. **creative**   Between Jackie and Ginny, Jackie is the _____.
                      (HINT: Careful! You are comparing only two people here!)

5. **hungry**   I am the _____ person in this class.

6. **quiet**   Lance is the _____ boy in the whole reading class.

7. **fantastic**   Harry Potter is one _____ kid.

8. **little**   The girl was _____ than her sister.

9. **far**   The sun is _____ away than the moon.

10. **patient**   Mrs. Hall is the _____ teacher I have ever had.

· ·

This homework is due at school on _____ .

_____   _____
         Child's signature   Parent's signature

Week-by-Week Homework for Building Grammar, Usage, and Mechanics Skills © 2010 by Mary Rose, Scholastic Teaching Resources

Name _____ Date _____

Directions: Read this story about the invention of the first video game, Pac-Man. Circle any boldfaced words that are incorrect. Make a correction in the space between the lines.

The History of Pac-Man

Do you like video games? Ever wonder what your parents **done** before video games were

invent? That was a long time ago. The first video game, Pac-Man, was invented in 1980.

A designer **naming** Tohru Iwatani went out for pizza. As he **removes** the first slice and **begins**

to eat, he noticed the pizza now looked like a head with an open mouth. Pac-Man was born!

Iwatani worked at a company called Namco. **Less** than nine people developed the game—

having Pac-Man go through a maze, eating dots until he dies. Pac-Man **have** "power pellets" to

get past things that tried to stop him. If he used his pellets **good**, he could go through the maze.

Pac-Man was played at an arcade. It cost 25 cents per game. The Pac-Man arcade game has

been played more than ten billion times in the last 20 to 30 years. That means it **have** made $100

million dollars, a quarter at a time!

There have been many "spin-offs" of the first Pac-Man. There were **newest** television shows and

most complicated video games. Companies made Pac-Man pasta, cereal, and T-shirts. There **is**

400 products with the Pac-Man logo and theme.

Some people were obsessed with Pac-Man. One man, Billy Mitchell, achieved the first perfect

score (3,333,360 points) after playing for six straight hours. It may not have been the **most**

healthiest use of time, but it made him famous.

I have had dreams of the Pac-Man chasing **myself**, but I am no longer afraid. Now, I am

waiting on the latest video game to come out!

✳ Answer Key

Section 1: Commas

Assessment: Commas

1. I used to live in **Phoenix,** Arizona.
2. Now I live in Salt Lake City.
3. **Hey, Michael,** would you like some candy?
4. St. Patrick's Day is always on March 17.
5. The **trick, of course,** is knowing where to throw the ball.
6. **Yes,** you may have some cookies.
7. We need to bring **crayons, scissors,** and glue to math class.
8. My teachers' names are **Miss Ridley, Mrs. Doerr,** and Mr. Sheldon.
9. **David,** could you take Emily fishing with you today?
10. **December 7, 1941,** is a famous date in our history.
11. I think our **principal, Mr. Morris,** is also great teacher.
12. I want to visit **New York, New Jersey, Maine,** and Vermont.
13. My brother signed the letter "**Sincerely,** George."
14. My cat is a **big, fat, old,** yellow stray.

Commas #1

Class Work

Answers will vary. Check that students put a comma between a city and a state, and between the day and year in a date.

Homework

I: Answers will vary. Check to be sure students put a comma between a city and a state, and between the day and the year in a date.
II: 1. incorrect 2. incorrect 3. correct 4. correct

Commas #2

Class Work

Add commas after: 1. pencils, eraser, notebooks 2. José, Kathy 3. puppy, goldfish, lizard 4. huge 5. large

Homework

I. Answers will vary. Check that students put a comma between words in a series.
II. 1. correct 2. incorrect 3. correct 4. incorrect

Commas #3

Class Work

Add commas after: 1. house 2. Well 3. out 4. lunch 5. door, Jake

Homework

I: Add commas after: 1. Sam 2. Okay 3. Lourdes 4. pool 5. vacation 6. yes
II: Add commas after: 1. Tim 2. yes, it, Joey 3. no commas 4. no commas 5. turtle, shells 6. yes, shell 7. Okay 8. no commas

Commas #4

Class Work

Add commas after: 1. Smith, teacher 2. teacher, Smith 3. Morris 4. Ivania, course 5. teacher, naturally

Homework

I: 1. child, obviously 2. yellow, naturally 3. no commas 4. do, then 5. prize, surprisingly
II: Paragraph 1 *commas after*: day, teacher, Conner, clay; **Paragraph 2** *commas after*: circles, old, metal, Next; *between* ribbon *and* which; *between* around *and* sort; **Paragraph 3** *commas after*: Next, Conner, patient, Finally, oven

Commas #5

Class Work

Responses will vary. Look for commas after the greeting and closing of the letter.

Homework

Add commas after: Helper, signed; Barbara, Sincerely; Helper, truly; Barbara, friend

Review: Commas

Letter 1 *commas after*: Waltz, 25, Burling, 1, 2007, Well, ago, not, course, young, Arezzo, harp, guitar, Finally, Waltz, student
Letter 2 *commas after*: Student, Neil, Guido, Lexington, Nebraska, 17, cook, garden, Wow, yours

Section 2: Apostrophes: Contractions & Possessives

Assessment: Apostrophes

I: 1. you will 2. do not 3. that is 4. I have 5. will not 6. Susan is 7. could not 8. it is
II: 1. isn't 2. haven't 3. he's 4. they're 5. aren't 6. wouldn't 7. there's 8. I'd
III: 1. Sue's cake 2. Jill's pail 3. Doug's pants 4. cats' toys 5. aunt's house

Apostrophes #1

Class Work

1. isn't 2. can't 3. weren't 4. shouldn't 5. won't

Homework

Write these words in the spaces: won't, haven't, don't, don't, wasn't, didn't, hadn't, isn't, couldn't, can't, doesn't

Apostrophes #2

Class Work

1. You've 2. It's 3. We've 4. Let's 5. They're 6. They'll

Homework

I: 1. I'll 2. You're 3. He's 4. You've 5. Who's 6. We're
II: 1. She will 2. They have 3. They will 4. It will 5. we will 6. Let us

Apostrophes #3

Class Work

Match these words and contractions: 1. you would, you'd; 2. I would, I'd; 3. she would, she'd; 4. could have, could've; 5. we would, we'd; 6. that would, that'd; 7. I had, I'd; 8. we had, we'd; 9. it had, it'd; 10. should have, should've

Homework

Write these words in the spaces: I'd; You'd; that'll; She'd; he'd; Who'd; you've; It'd; that'll; they'd; you've; that'd; I'd

Apostrophes #4

Class Work

1. possession 2. possession 3. contraction 4. contraction 5. possession 6. contraction

Homework

I. 1. contraction 2. possession 3. possession 4. possession 5. possession 6. contraction
II. 1. contraction 2. possession 3. possession 4. possession 5. contraction 6. contraction

Apostrophes #5

Class Work

1. Circle *haven't* and *no*. Rewrite: They have no mail this morning. (circle *no*); They haven't gotten any mail this morning. (circle *haven't*)
2. Circle *isn't* and *nowhere*. Rewrite: Bill is going nowhere today. (circle *nowhere*); Bill isn't going anywhere today. (circle *isn't*)
3. Circle *hasn't* and *nobody*. Rewrite: Sheila has nobody to talk to. (circle *nobody*); Sheila hasn't got anybody to talk to. (circle *hasn't*)
4. Circle *isn't* and *nothing*. Rewrite: There is nothing you can do about the weather. (circle *nothing*); There isn't anything you can do about the weather. (circle *isn't*)

Homework

1. Circle *hasn't* and *never*. Rewrite: That dog has never barked at a stranger. (circle *never*); That dog hasn't ever barked at a stranger. (circle *hasn't*)
2. Circle *haven't* and *none*. Rewrite: I have none left. (circle *none*); I haven't any left. (circle *haven't*)
3. Circle *isn't* and *no*. Rewrite: There is no one at home today. (circle *no*); There isn't anyone at home today. (circle *isn't*)
4. Circle *hardly* and *don't*. Rewrite: I have hardly any time these days. (circle *hardly*); I don't have any time these days. (circle *don't*)
5. Circle *don't* and *nothing*. Rewrite: They have nothing to wear to the party. (circle *nothing*) They don't have anything to wear to the party. (circle *don't*)

Review: Apostrophes

I: 1. that is 2. they would 3. she is 4. you have 5. it will 6. who is 7. you have 8. must not 9. Linda is 10. did not
II: 1. baby's toys 2. won't 3. we'd 4. didn't 5. students' essays 6. what's 7. he'll 8. they've 9. Markeshia's 10. we've

Section 3: Quotations & Quotation Marks

Assessment: Quotations

I. 1. none: movie title 2. "The Itsy, Bitsy Spider" 3. none: book title 4. "Happy Birthday!" 5. "When I grow up," said Alma, "I want to be a scientist." 6. Sabrina said, "When I grow up, I want to be a nurse. I want to help sick children."
II. 1. "I want a pony for my birthday," said

Kathryn.   2. "I don't want a pony," said William. "I want a dog."   3. "Why would you want a dog?" asked Kathryn. "You can't ride a dog."   4. "I want a dog because I can sleep with him. You can't sleep with a pony," explained William.

Quotations #1

Class Work

Use quotation marks as follows: "The Boy Who Lived"; "Tattooin' Ruth"; "The Tell-Tale Heart"; "The Adventure of the Red-Headed League"

Homework

Use quotation marks as follows: "The Mysterious Black Cat"; "I Waited Too Long"; "I Ate Too Much"; "The New Kid"; "You Raise Me Up"

Quotations #2

Class Work

Exact words: *It is time for lunch.* Punctuate: "It is time for lunch," said Mrs. Baker; Exact words: *We are hungry.* Punctuate: The children said, "We are hungry." Circle *I* in *It*; *W* in *We*.

Homework

Luis said, "I really want a puppy." Circle *I*.

Mother said, "You cannot have a dog." Circle *Y* in *You*.

Luis said, "Maurice has puppies for sale." Circle *M* in *Maurice*.

Mother said, "I know Maurice has puppies for sale." Circle *I*.

"They are only twenty-five dollars," said Luis. Circle *T* in *They*.

"Do you have twenty-five dollars?" asked Mother. Circle *D* in *Do*.

"No, I don't have twenty-five dollars," said Luis. Circle *N* in *No*.

"Then how will you buy a puppy?" asked Mother. Circle *T* in *Then*.

Luis smiled and said, "I thought you would buy one for me." Circle *I*.

Mother smiled back and said, "You thought wrong, Luis." Circle *Y* in *You*.

Then Father was standing in the doorway.

"Maybe Father will buy a puppy for me," said Luis. Circle *M* in *Maybe*.

"You won't get a puppy if your mother says no," said Father. Circle *Y* in *You*.

"May I get one if I save my own money?" asked Luis. Circle *M* in *May*.

Father and Mother said, "Twenty-five dollars is a lot of money. We'll see." Circle *T* in *Twenty-five*.

Quotations #3

Class Work

1. "I think," said Mrs. Rodriguez, "that we should have a special reading class today."

2. "What," asked the children, "will we do differently?"

3. "Well," explained the teacher, "we will have our reading class under the big oak tree."

4. "Hurrah! Mrs. Rodriguez," cheered the children, "you are the best!"

Homework

1. "Today is a good day," Mrs. Chiu explained, "for getting a class pet."

2. "Yes," shouted the children, "that would be a great idea!"

3. "Well," asked Mrs. Chiu, "what pet do you think we should get?"

4. "I think," answered Jerry, "we should get mice."

5. "Okay," agreed Mrs. Chiu, "mice will be the perfect pets for our classroom."

Quotations #4

Class Work

Mrs. Sanders said, "You are not going to believe where we are going on our field trip. You are going to love this!"

"Where, where, where?" asked every child in the class.

"I'm not going to tell you," replied Mrs. Sanders. "I'm going to see if you can guess."

"Give us a hint," begged the children. "Give us a big, big hint."

"We are staying in Orlando," explained Mrs. Baker. "We are going to EPCOT."

"We are going to Disney World!" shouted the children.

"We are," said Mrs. Sanders. "Disney is letting all fourth graders in Florida visit free. We even get a free lunch."

"We can't wait!" yelled the children. "Disney World is the happiest place on Earth!"

Homework

"Who is the greatest NASCAR driver of all time?" asked Jordan. "Do you have a clue?"

"I don't know," I replied. "Could it be Jeff Gordon?"

"No," said Jordan. "It is Richard Petty."

"I have heard of him," I said. "What makes him so great?"

"You don't know?" exclaimed Jordan. "Do you live in a cave? How many wins does Jeff Gordon have?"

"Jeff Gordon has 92 wins, almost a record," I bragged.

"Well, if it is ALMOST a record, who holds the record for all-time NASCAR wins? Do you have a clue now?"

"I don't know," I stammered. "I guess the answer might be Richard Petty. How many wins does he have?"

"Are you ready for this?" asked Jordan. "Richard Petty has 200 wins. What do you think of that?"

"I think that is pretty impressive," I said. "Boy, I know why they always refer to him as 'The King.'"

Quotations #5

Class Work

P "Did you ever hear of the Little League World Series?" asked Lee. "It is held each summer in Cooperstown, New York." P "Why do they hold it clear up there?" asked Isabelle. P "They do it there because that is the location of the Baseball Hall of Fame," replied Lee. P Isabelle and Lee are brother and sister. Lee was chosen to play first base in the series. "I hope you win a big trophy," said Isabelle.

Homework

P "I'm going to a meeting and will be back in five minutes," said my teacher, Mr. Smith. P As he left, he propped a paper bag up on his desk. About five minutes later, the bag moved. The whole class looked up. P "Go touch it," said a girl sitting next to me. P "OK," I said. P I pushed my chair out from my desk and got up. I walked over to the desk and poked the bag. It started moving again. Then I opened it. There was a little animal, but it was only a couple of inches tall. It raised its arms, and I picked it up. P Jacquez screamed, "AHHHH! Are you crazy, Michael?" P I looked back inside the bag. There was a little chest small enough to fit in the palm of a hand. P "I wonder what that is," I thought. P Then I saw the animal I had taken out of the bag. It had grown, but not just a little bit! It was as big as my desk. P The only thing I could find in my voice was "Oh, no!" P I ran to the bag and opened the chest. There was honey in it. I fed it to the animal. Just then, Mr. Smith walked in. P "What are you doing?" asked Mr. Smith. P "Mr. Smith," I said, smiling my nicest smile. "Was this supposed to be for science class?"

Review: Quotations

P "Please take these papers to the office," said Mrs. Miller. P I picked up the papers and started out of the door. P "And hurry back because it is almost time for our math test." P "OK," I said. P I was just walking down the hallway to the office, when I noticed that my shoe was untied. I bent down to tie it and noticed a small door. It was right beside the drinking fountain, but I had never noticed it before. I stooped down and went through it. P "What are you doing in here?" cried a loud voice. "No children are allowed here in the teachers' lounge." P I knew I was in trouble when I saw it was Mr. Merkle. P "I am so sorry," I said. "I was looking for the office. How do I get out of here?" P "First, you give me that book, young man." P "What book? I am just taking papers to the office for Mrs. Miller." P "I don't see any papers. I only see a copy of a short story by Sherlock Holmes. Where did you get that? I am missing a copy of this book from my classroom." P "I have no idea, Mr. Merkle. I only know that I went through a little door." P "Well, you had best get back through that door right now." P I walked slowly toward the soda machine and was suddenly back in the hallway tying my shoe. I looked down and saw Mrs. Miller's papers. I hurried to the office and then back to class just in time to hear, "Get out a paper and pencil for the math test." P What a crazy day!

Section 4: **Capitalization**

Assessment: Capitalization

1. Northeast 2. northeast 3. Street 4. ocean 5. Atlantic Ocean 6. burger 7. Uncle 8. uncle 9. Doctor (or Dr.) 10. doctor 11. Valentine's Day 12. Sandy 13. Oregon 14. November 15. October; month

Capitalization #1

Class Work

1. Doctor (or Dr.) Smith 2. Omaha, Nebraska 3. I, Dallas, Texas 4. George, Chicago, cat, Pebbles 5. sister, Susan

Homework

What is the number-one *fast-food* chain in the world? If you guessed *McDonald's*, then *you* guessed right. A man named *Mr. Ray Kroc* opened the first *McDonald's* restaurant in 1955. It was in *Des Plaines*, *Illinois* near *Chicago*. He wanted to train his *workers* to be clean, friendly, and *organized*, so he opened a school called *Hamburger University*. At first, he sold his *hamburgers* for 15 cents. Now, people all over the world enjoy *McDonald's* food. Today there are *restaurants* in 100 countries, including *India* and *China*. In *America*, we love to visit *fast-food* restaurants—and the one with the golden *arches* is our favorite.

Capitalization #2

Class Work

Answers 1–3 will vary. Be sure students use capital letters for the names of months, holidays, days of the week, and to begin sentences. 4. Summer months: June, July, August; 5. Fall holidays: Columbus Day, Halloween, Veterans Day, Thanksgiving

Homework

Italicized words should be uppercase.

National Peanut Day is celebrated on *September* 13. *Actually*, peanuts are not nuts. *They* are called "*legumes*," and are like peas and beans. *Peanuts* are quite good for you. *They* are high in protein and fiber, and because they fill you up quickly, you tend to eat less. *You* may want to celebrate this day and also *National Peanut Butter Lovers' Day* on *March* 1st. *In* 2011, *National Peanut Butter Lovers' Day* will be on a *Tuesday*. *It* will be the perfect day for you to get out a jar of *Jif* or *Peter Pan* peanut butter and make yourself a sandwich. *Don't* forget the grape jelly!

Capitalization #3

Class Work

1. Bridge 2. bridge 3. pond 4. Pond 5. Lake 6. lake 7. road 8. Road

Homework

1. building 2. Building 3. Park 4. park 5. bank 6. Bank 7. River 8. river 9. queen 10. Queen 11. street, Street 12. field 13. Field 14. Ocean 15. ocean

Capitalization #4

Class Work

1. correct 2. correct 3. correct 4. correct 5. incorrect: grandmother

Homework

1. correct 2. incorrect: Grandmother 3. correct 4. correct 5. incorrect: Grandfather 6. correct 7. correct 8. correct 9. correct 10. incorrect: father 11. incorrect: nephew 12. correct

Capitalization #5

Class Work

1. southern 2. Midwest 3. north 4. North 5. northeastern 6. north, south

Homework

1. Northwest 2. east, west 3. southernmost 4. East, West 5. Southwest 6. South 7. south 8. Midwest 9. midwestern 10. North 11. east 12. northern 13. Southeast 14. north 15. south

Capitalization Review

Pennsylvania is located in the *Northeast*. The *state* has 45,000 square miles of land, and the capital is *Harrisburg*. It is famous for *livestock* and *steel*.

Oklahoma is located in the *center* of our country. It has the *National Cowboy Hall of Fame*.

The *state fair* is held in *September* each year.

Texas is located *south* of *Oklahoma*. *Texas* is the home of the *Alamo*. On *Tuesday, February 23, 1836*, there was a battle that made this building famous.

Vermont is the *Green Mountain State*. My *sister* lives there. I go for a visit every *summer*, but this year, *I* am going at *Christmastime*.

California is one of our largest *states*. It is in the *western* part of the *United States*.

Section 5: Spelling

Assessment: Spelling

1. separate 2. there 3. knife 4. answer 5. bridge 6. see, sea 7. believe 8. your 9. sign 10. Tomorrow 11. Our/hour 12. principal 13. often 14. you're 15. their

Spelling #1

Class Work

1. there 2. their 3. their 4. there 5. They're

Homework

1. they're 2. their 3. there 4. there 5. their 6. They're 7. there 8. their 9. their 10. They're

Spelling #2

Class Work

1. your 2. You're 3. Your 4. You're, your 5. your, your 6. you're, your

Homework

1. your 2. you're 3. you're, your 4. your 5. You're, your 6. your 7. your, your 8. your, you're 9. your 10. your 11. you're 12. your

Spelling #3

Class Work

1. salmon 2. bridge 3. high 4. ghost 5. knee 6. bought, Depot

Homework

1. island 2. caught 3. comb 4. foreign 5. sign 6. answer 7. autumn 8. debt 9. bought 10. honest

Spelling #4

Class Work

1. blue, blew 2. eight, ate 3. piece, peace 4. flour, flower 5. sale, sail 6. cent, sent, scent

Homework

1. heel, heal 2. threw, through 3. weak, week 4. Tale, tail 5. brake, break 6. hear, here 7. seen, scene 8. to, too, two

Spelling #5

Class Work

Answers will vary.

Homework

1. thief 2. separate 3. chocolate 4. weird 5. principal 6. vacuum 7. Tomorrow

Review: Spelling

I: February, tomorrow, separate, believe, Wednesday, calendar, weird, vacuum, honest, bridge, doubt, knife

II: 1. their 2. there 3. you're 4. your 5. they're

II: ate, eight 2. blue, blew 3. piece 4. threw, through 5. claws

Section 6: **Word Choice**

Assessment: Word Choice

I: 1. called 2. said 3. came 4. ran
II: 1. hope 2. are 3. needs 4. hopes
III: 1. May 2. well 3. me 4. fewer
IV: 1. coldest 2. colder 3. dangerous 4. more dangerous

Word Choice #1

Class Work

Answers may vary but should be similar to these: *The teacher listened yesterday. The teacher is listening now. The teacher will listen tomorrow.*

Homework

Answers will vary. Students should write three sentences for each verb, one in the past, present and future, using the subjects and verbs given.

Word Choice #2

Class Work

Students should draw lines to match these words: know, knew; pay, paid; read, read; freeze, froze; drive, drove; catch, caught; fall, fell; write, wrote; think, thought; swing, swung

Homework

I. Students should draw lines to match these words: hide, hid; leave, left; bring, brought; lose, lost; sing, sang; stand, stood; swim, swam; give, gave; draw, drew; keep, kept

II. began; caught; cut; taught; thought; shook; broke; drank; held; slid

Word Choice #3

Class Work

1. **P:** were 2. **P:** are 3. **S:** is 4. **S:** am 5. **P:** hit 6. **S:** hits 7. **P:** read 8. **S:** reads

Homework

I: 1. **S:** whispers 2. **P:** whisper 3. **P:** watch 4. **S:** watches 5. **S:** thinks 6. **P:** think

II. Answers will vary. Check sentences for subject-verb agreement.

Word Choice #4

No Class Work responses.

Homework

1. May, can 2. Wait for, wait on 3. less, fewer 4. well, good 5. healthy, healthful 6. me, myself 7. fewer, less 8. I, myself

Word Choice #5

Class Work

1. wet; wetter 2. warm; warmer; warmest 3. sunny; sunnier; sunniest 4. cooperative; more cooperative; most cooperative 5. colorful; more colorful; most colorful

Homework

1. soft, softer, softest 2. comfortable, more comfortable, most comfortable 3. more playful 4. more creative 5. hungriest 6. quietest 7. fantastic 8. littler 9. farther 10. most patient

Review: Word Choice

Change these words: *done* to *did*; *invent* to *invented*; *naming* to *named*; *removes* to *removed*; *begins* to *began*; *less* to *fewer*; *have* to *had*; *good* to *well*; *have* to *has*; *newest* to *new*; *most* to *more*; *is* to *are*; *most healthiest* to *most healthful*; *myself* to *me*; *waiting on* to *waiting for*